# Stewardship

# Stewardship
## Living a Biblical Call

Bernard F. Evans

**LITURGICAL PRESS**
Collegeville, Minnesota

www.litpress.org

Cover design by Ann Blattner. Illustration courtesy of Thinkstock by Getty Images.

Scripture texts in this work are taken from the *New Revised Standard Version Bible: Catholic Edition* © 1989, 1993, Division of Christian Education of the National Council of the Churches of Christ in the United States of America. Used by permission. All rights reserved.

Excerpts from documents of the Second Vatican Council are from *Vatican Council II: Constitutions, Decrees, Declarations—The Basic Sixteen Documents*, edited by Austin Flannery, OP © 1996. Used with permission of Liturgical Press, Collegeville, Minnesota.

1    2    3    4    5    6    7    8    9

**Library of Congress Cataloging-in-Publication Data**

Evans, Bernard F., 1943–
      Stewardship : living a biblical call / Bernard F. Evans.
         pages cm
      ISBN 978-0-8146-3425-7 — ISBN 978-0-8146-3426-4 (ebook)
      1. Christian stewardship.    I. Title.

BV772.E93 2014
248'.6—dc23                                                        2014001608

To the Basilica of Saint Mary (Minneapolis),
whose pastoral leadership, staff, and volunteers
so faithfully and effectively model
biblical stewardship

# Contents

# Introduction

In the Gospel of Luke (12:16-21) Jesus tells the parable of a rich man whose crops were abundant and required larger storage bins. So the man tore down the old and built new ones, and then rejoiced that he had plenty of goods to last him many years and now he could "relax, eat, drink, be merry." But that night his life ended.

This parable is not just about the uncertainty of life and the time of our death. It is especially about our relationship with God and how that relationship is formed by our attitude toward the things we own and the talents and abilities we enjoy. The story of the rich man raises particularly challenging questions about how we are to use these gifts as well as the many resources we come to possess throughout our lives.

It is these questions that this book addresses while exploring the biblical and theological meaning of stewardship. The Scriptures speak often and deeply about how we might respond to these questions, about how our standing with God is shaped by the way we utilize the gifts and resources with which God has blessed us. So do the earliest Christian theologians as they reflect on what it means to be a disciple of Jesus Christ during the first four centuries. Fast-forward to modern times and we find that Catholic social teachings have much to say about ownership and use of our possessions as well. These three sources—the Bible, early Christian writers, and modern Catholic social teachings—provide the material for this book's reflection on stewardship, on how we are to use the gifts and resources God has presented to us.

The first part of the book addresses the general foundations of biblical stewardship. It considers creation as a whole and our obligation to take care of what belongs to God while finding

1

our place within the created order (chap. 1). This part recognizes the general obligation to care for all people—ourselves and all of God's children (chap. 2). Finally, part 1 presents stewardship as a matter of justice (chap. 3). Sharing God's resources and the talents God has placed within each of us is an expectation of biblical justice.

The second part explores various forms of stewardship, more specific ways to think about and practice the general biblical call to live stewardship. "Personal Stewardship" (chap. 4) discusses how we respond to God's call by developing the gifts God has placed within us. "Stewardship of Our Gifts" (chap. 5) considers how we are to serve one another by following Jesus' own example of love and service. "Local Stewardship" (chap. 6) speaks of loving God by loving, in practical ways, the neighbor who is in front of us. "Global Stewardship" (chap. 7) struggles with the challenge of loving the more distant neighbor, the one we will never meet. "Ecological Stewardship" (chap. 8) engages the obvious challenge of being good stewards of God's wondrous creation. Finally, "Financial Stewardship" (chap. 9) considers sharing our monetary resources, and doing so for the right motive.

Each chapter ends with a brief section titled "Getting Practical." The purpose of these sections is to provide down-to-earth practical suggestions on how, in our busy and demanding lives, we might live out the biblical call to stewardship in relation to the topic of the chapter. These suggestions are minimal and readers surely will come up with more and better ways to practice stewardship in the context of their own lives. The "Getting Practical" sections aim to offer a few directions for acting or living stewardship, but also to affirm that there are many ways for stewardship to become an everyday part of our lives.

Stewardship, then, is not primarily about giving money. Certainly it includes that, but it is at its core an attitude and a habit of using all the gifts and abilities God has granted us. That includes having the right attitude about the material things we own. The rich man in Luke's gospel kept building bigger storage bins. Jesus presented this parable to remind us that we have other options.

# PART I

# 1

# Creation

The earth is the Lord's and all that is in it,
the world, and those who live in it.

—Psalm 24:1

Creation—the wondrous work of God, the playground of our lives, the starting point for our contact with God. Creation also is the entry point to our discussion of what Scripture says about stewardship, about using the gifts God has placed within us and around us. For it is here, within the rest of creation, that we define our relationship with God and with our neighbor. How we look at creation, how we see ourselves as belonging to this creation, leads us to know that everything we are, everything we possess, everything we become is because of God. This evolving appreciation of our place within creation molds the simple but firm conviction that we must care for all that God has made.

## Creation Is God's

All of creation is God's, even our own lives. We speak of the right to life, and we acknowledge the care and compassion we owe to other human beings. We accept the general norm that in daily living no one has the right to take the life of another person. Human life is sacred and its ending should be the result of a natural process, not the action of another member of the human family.

But we also know that our lives are pure gift from God. None of us can claim that we have a right to continue living, as if life is something God owes us. We live simply because God has lovingly willed us to live. Everything within creation, including our lives, belongs to God—"The earth is the Lord's and all that is in it, / the world, and those who live in it." The psalmist could not have been clearer: creation is God's.

It is not surprising that many of the earliest Christian writers repeated and developed this biblical claim in language and images that spoke to Christians of their day. The first-century *Didache* offered a brief instruction on Christian living for persons who wished to become members of the earliest Christian communities. This "Teaching of the Twelve Apostles" explained what it means for followers of Jesus Christ to live the Way of Life. Striving to live this life, for example, must include a willingness to share one's possessions with persons who have little or none:

> Do not turn away from the needy, but share all with your brother and do not claim that it is your own. For, if you are sharers in immortal things, how much more in mortal.[1]

The *Didache* reminded future Christians that earthly possessions are not entirely their own. Everything belongs to God and must be used to glorify God through proper use.

Later in the second century St. Irenaeus of Lyons emphasized that point while commenting on what proper use of our possessions requires:

> It is necessary, then, that we begin with the first and greatest principle, with the Creator God who made heaven and earth and all things in them.[2]

If we are clear on that starting point, we are less likely to lose our way in making sound judgments about the use and applications of our many gifts. But we must not forget who the owner is of all that we possess, use, and enjoy throughout our lives.

Around that same time St. Basil addressed the expectation that Christians share their goods with persons who lack what they need for living a decent life. In his homilies he scolded those Christians who seemed unwilling to share from their abundance. Such persons, he said, suffer a loss of memory. They forget that they are stewards, not owners of what they possess. Creation is made by God and belongs to God. Our use of all that God provides must reflect this fundamental biblical principle: "The earth is the LORD's and all that is in it."

For the Hebrew people their interaction with the land was an especially important place to live out this biblical sense of stewardship. The book of Leviticus is particularly clear when it instructs the Israelites regarding their tenure on the land:

> The land shall not be sold in perpetuity, for the land is mine; with me you are but aliens and tenants. (25:23)

Land held great importance for the Hebrew people—as it does for their descendants today. It was the promise to Abraham, Isaac, and Jacob. It was the task of Moses to lead the Israelites to the land God was giving them. Yet even in that sacred place they were to see themselves as strangers and guests ("aliens and tenants") upon this land. It is not theirs; it belongs to God.

That message is embedded in the sabbatical laws found in the book of Exodus:

> For six years you shall sow your land and gather in its yield; but the seventh year you shall let it rest and lie fallow, so that the poor of your people may eat; and what they leave the wild animals may eat. You shall do the same with your vineyard, and with your olive orchard. (23:10-11)

Here too is a reminder to the people that the land—in which they now live and from which they receive food—belongs to God and is theirs only to use. Even in their use of this land, the people are to share its fruits with those among them who are poor, and with the rest of God's creatures ("the wild animals may eat"). As they use what is given for their own sustenance the people of Israel must consider how this abundance might serve the needs of others besides themselves—other people and other species. This inclusive attitude regarding who should benefit from God's creation, this humble recognition that it is not entirely for or about humans, likely positioned the Hebrew people to act as good stewards of the land and, in doing so, to honor the God who brought it into existence and guided them to it.

The Scriptures also suggest that the land—and all of creation—enjoys its own relationship with the Creator:

> When you enter the land that I am giving you, the land shall observe a sabbath for the LORD. Six years you shall sow your field, and six years you shall prune your vineyard, and gather in their yield; but in the seventh year there shall be a sabbath of complete rest for the land, a sabbath for the LORD: you shall not sow your field or prune your vineyard. (Lev 25:2-4)

So among the Sabbath laws there is one for the land. The land shall observe a year of rest and, as with the people, this time of rest is a time devoted to the Lord. It shall be "a sabbath for the LORD." Creation has its own relationship with God, one not dependent on human mediation.

Psalm 148 jubilantly summons all creation to praise the Lord, to rejoice in that relationship:

> Praise him, sun and moon;
>     praise him, all you shining stars!
> Praise him, you highest heavens,
>     and you waters above the heavens!
> Let them praise the name of the LORD,
>     for he commanded and they were created. (vv. 3-5)

Sun and moon, water and sea creatures; fire, hail, and snow; mountains and hills; trees, beasts, and birds—all should praise the God of creation. To God they owe their sustenance, their beauty, their life. In return they offer praise to their Creator, the God to whom they belong and in whom they delight.

In modern society we often look upon the rest of creation as having value only insofar as it benefits humans. We drain wetlands so that farmers can plant crops and make that land useful and productive. We level mountains so that mining companies can extract deposits of coal needed to fire the great furnaces that heat our buildings. We spray our lawns so that we can enjoy only green grass on the little piece of creation we claim as our own. Our attitude toward nature sometimes reflects a mistaken view that creation is of our making and that its sole purpose is to serve us. The one Creator of this world occasionally reminds us that we humans may not be the only reason for his handiwork and, further, that we cannot understand how it all works.

In the book of Job we find a stunning reminder of this and of the fact that our God is the Lord of all creation. Job experiences what feels like an unending series of tragic misfortunes. His servants are attacked and killed; his livestock are stolen; his children are killed when a mighty wind brings down their house. Job complains to God that there is something unfair about all his suffering; he is, after all, a righteous man. He questions whether a God of justice would inflict an upright man with so much loss and grief. God answers Job with a series of questions about who is the Creator and who is the creature:

> Where were you when I laid the foundation of the earth?
>   Tell me, if you have understanding.
> Who determined its measurements—surely you know!
>   Or who stretched the line upon it?
> On what were its bases sunk,
>   or who laid its cornerstone
> when the morning stars sang together
>   and all the heavenly beings shouted for joy? (38:4-7)

In responding to Job's doubts about God's justice, God does not enter into a debate about divine justice. He does not even answer the questions Job puts forward. God simply reminds this human that he, God, is the Creator of all. Little more needs to be said.

Questioning God—or God's justice—in the midst of tragedy continues to this day. We wonder aloud how a loving God can allow innocent people to die in tornadoes or car accidents or street gang shoot-outs. Yet even in such moments we also hear people express a recognition that their lives and possessions belong to the Creator. Survivors of a fire or natural disaster often express a deep-felt gratitude that they are able to live on even when their homes and possessions have been destroyed. This may be a moment of great loss in their lives but it can also become a transforming realization of how dependent they are on God for everything they possess, including their lives.

Such moments may reveal another human characteristic. Deep within us is an awareness rarely articulated that everything in our world owes its existence to God and belongs to God. Even as we gather possessions or build financial empires we have to know that none of it goes with us into the next life. We might plan for our wealth or possessions or businesses to pass to our children. We may will some of what we own to be taken over by one charity or another when we die. Those very actions, however, are a de facto recognition that our material goods, including those we have worked so hard to acquire, belong to another. The intense and busy nature of our lives allows us to ignore for the moment this and many other truths about our lives and about the rest of creation. Sometimes we need to be reminded through the fear of a natural disaster or through a Job-like experience that it is all God's and it is all about God.

## Finding Our Place within God's Creation

If creation belongs to God, what is our place within it? Do we have a role different from other living beings? Is there anything that sets us apart from the squirrels, the skunks, and the chipmunks? What did God have in mind for us?

The Scriptures have much to say about this but two creation stories are particularly helpful in addressing these questions. Both stories are from the opening pages of the Bible. Each was written at a different time in the history of Israel and each carries its own message about Israel's understanding of God and of the peoples' relationship to this God. Although these creation stories were not concerned about twenty-first-century environmental problems, the two accounts provide striking insights on humankind's relationship to the rest of creation—on humankind's place within this garden that God has planted.

The first of these stories represents the most familiar account of our role among the other creatures. Through much of human history we have used this story—especially the following verses—to establish humankind's superiority over everything else that God has made:

> So God created humankind in his image,
>     in the image of God he created them;
>     male and female he created them.
> God blessed them and God said to them, "Be fruitful and multiply, and fill the earth and subdue it; and have dominion over the fish of the sea and over the birds of the air and over every living thing that moves upon the earth." (Gen 1:27-28)

Throughout this entire story, which encompasses all of the first chapter of the first book of the Bible, no other creature or part of creation enjoys this unique status. Humans alone are made in the image of God. Male and female God created them, and God blessed them.

Our understanding of what it means to be made in God's image has developed in Christian theology over the centuries. Through much of this history our likeness to the Creator was seen in humans' ability to reason, to understand, and to make choices—in our intellect and will. More contemporary reflections on this special status of humans tend to focus on our ability to enter into loving and caring relationships with others. In this we reflect our likeness to the divine Creator. However we understand being made in God's image, in the first creation story it is clear that humans alone enjoy this special status of reflecting in some way the likeness of God.

This creation story from Genesis 1 also makes the point that humans are to exercise dominion over all other living beings: "over every living thing that moves upon the earth." Too often in human history this text has been understood as granting people the authority to do whatever they wish to the natural world. According to that line of thought God not only created the world for humans to use but also put humans in charge, giving us the right to treat the rest of creation any way we see fit. Obviously this way of interpreting the "have dominion over" text is problematic.

Our concern today about climate change and other environmental problems begs us to reexamine this ancient text in light of contemporary human experience. We can name too many examples of human behavior toward nature that can only be characterized as abusive. Excessive applications of nitrate fertilizer on Midwestern farm fields results in a massive dead zone in the Gulf of Mexico depriving all species of fish the oxygen necessary for life. Is this what it means to "have dominion over"? Scientific experimentation in human reproduction holds the possibility of cloning humans. Is this how we are to exercise our special place within creation? Is the rest of creation here simply for our experimentation and enjoyment?

Indeed, biblical scholarship cautions against a strictly human-centered reading of the creation story in Genesis 1. To have dominion over is more accurately read as a call to stewardship. That is, humans are given the responsibility of taking care of what belongs to God. To have dominion over means to watch over the rest of creation as God would, in the place of God. What would it look like if we were to care for creation as God would?

To answer that question we need to appreciate that the Hebrew people understood their God as a God with a special love and concern for the poor, the defenseless, and the vulnerable. This was, after all, the God who led them from slavery in Egypt to freedom in the land once promised to Abraham. So to watch over any part of creation in the place of God necessarily meant treating the natural world with the same love and compassion that Yahweh showed toward them. This does not mean that humans cannot use and enjoy other living things in the natural world. It does suggest, however, that we do so with an awareness of the responsibility God has given us, and with a reverence for all life—human and others—that reflects the beauty and love of the Creator.

In reflecting on humans' special status some early Christian theologians offered an insight both humbling and enriching. Humankind's unique position among all of God's creatures is for the sake of the rest of creation, so that all we regard as earthly might be elevated to the divine. For some this might grant too much to humans—a mediating role between creation and God—but it certainly finds support among early Christian writers.

Saint Gregory of Nazianzus, for example, observed how suited humans are to carry out this role. Man is

> king of the things on earth yet ruled from above, earthly and heavenly, subject to time yet deathless, visible and knowable, standing halfway between greatness and lowliness. He is at the same time spirit and flesh: spirit because of grace, flesh because of pride—the one, that he might always remain in being and glorify his benefactor; the other that he might suffer, and in his suffering come to his senses, and be corrected from his ambitions of grandeur. He is a living being: cared for in this world, transferred to another, and, as the final stage of the mystery, made divine by his inclination towards God.[3]

Humans' unique role within the created order allows us to perceive God's wisdom and purposes in creation, to reflect some likeness to God, and to honor this Creator of all through our careful and compassionate guardianship of the natural world. Thus, we not only exercise some form of dominion or stewardship over the other creatures but we also recognize the mystery of this creation in which we participate as fellow members of the created order.

The second creation story provides a balance or check on any tendency to grant humans too lofty a place within God's creation. It allows humans the role of naming "every living creature," which in ancient times signified a measure of authority on the part of the one doing the naming. At the same time, in what else it says, and does not say, this story reminds us that we humans are primarily a part of this creation that God told us to watch over. There is no mention of us being made in the likeness of God. Nor are humans told to have dominion over all other living beings. Rather the text points out how much we are like the other creatures:

> [T]hen the LORD God formed man from the dust of the ground . . . Out of the ground the LORD God made to grow every tree . . . So out of the ground the LORD God formed every animal of the field and every bird of the air. (Gen 2:7, 9, 19)

In this account of creation humans are made of the same stuff as the trees, animals, and birds. There is no suggestion of us being fashioned in the likeness of God. We are just made—like everything else—from the ground. From the moment of our coming into being we are connected to all other living things. We are part of creation.

Indeed, humans carry a special role, a unique responsibility within creation. We are not the same as the squirrels, skunks, and chipmunks. The Creator of all has chosen to place upon humans the responsibility of looking out for the rest of creation. He has endowed us with the gifts and capacities to do so. It is our goal to till and to keep the garden in the place of the one who made it all come into being.

But we also are part of that creation, part of that created order. Though made in God's image and enjoying a sacred dignity not granted to any other of God's creatures, we remain more creature than creator. In that way our similarity with those squirrels is assured.

There are many other places in the Bible where we can find direction on how we should regard nature and all the world around us. There are other biblical texts reminding us that creation belongs to God and that our role here is one of grateful stewards. One such text is Deuteronomy 14:22, one of the most popular biblical references to tithing within Christian churches:

> Set apart a tithe of all the yield of your seed that is brought in yearly from the field.

The tithe referenced here—and in Numbers 18:21-32 and Leviticus 27:30-33—is an offering consistent with the biblical practice of presenting to God the firstfruits, whether produce from the field or livestock from the herd. Offering the tithe was an important way of acknowledging that we have this sheep or this grain because of God. It is God who sent the rains and made the soil fertile. Without God's abundantly rich land, water, and favorable climates, none of us could make anything grow.

In the biblical context, our tithe is a simple but direct acknowledgment that this produce, upon which our lives depend, is available to us because of our loving, caring God. So, our offering to God is not because God needs it, but because we need to remind ourselves how dependent we are on God for the most fundamental elements of our continued existence. And, all these gifts and resources in nature that nourish us and allow us to flourish—all of this—belongs to God. This is the beginning of stewardship.

## ✒ Getting Practical

### Growing Our Relationship with God in the Midst of God's Creation

The beginning of stewardship is recognizing that everything within creation belongs to God. How we bring this truth into our lives will shape how we choose to use the many gifts God has granted us. We need to be clear on what this means for our own lives, for our developing relationship with God, and for how we use the material possessions we refer to as "ours." There are a number of practical approaches we might take to appreciating more clearly the biblical insights on creation and our place within it.

### It Is God's

If all of creation belongs to God, what does this mean for how we live our lives on a daily basis, freely using the gifts of nature like clean air and water? These simple but essential elements of nature are gifts from our Creator that we cannot live without. How easily we take these for granted with little thought about who provides them. A good practice would be to reflect on this from time to time as a way of remembering how dependent we are on the Creator who so generously provides these and all the other resources upon which we as individuals and as a human community rely. This kind of grateful reflection can enrich our ever-developing relationship with God and do so in relation to this beautiful world we are blessed to enjoy and called to protect.

When we acknowledge that "the earth is the LORD's and all that is in it," how does this affect or shape our thinking about our own possessions? In our society private ownership stands as a near sacred institution. We take it for granted that all people have the right to own privately whatever their resources allow them to purchase. This may be one of those areas where the biblical teaching on creation is not an easy fit for modern Western thinking on private ownership. The two may not contradict each other, but they certainly require careful adjusting. All of us would benefit from some clarifying reading and reflection on how we should regard our possessions. A helpful resource on this is Catholic social teaching that recognizes the right to private ownership (On the Condition of Labor, Pope Leo XIII, 1891) but also sets limits and expectations for how we use whatever we own (On the Development of Peoples, Pope Paul VI, 1967).

*Our Place within Creation*

The Scriptures tell us that humans are given dominion over the rest of creation. We know this is not a license to abuse, destroy, or even do whatever we wish to God's beautiful planet. It is, rather, a summons to look after and care for God's world. Our responsibility is to care for all of creation as God would—with love and compassion and with a special sensitivity to that which is vulnerable and easily hurt.

But what does it mean to be stewards of the earth at this time? Today we are facing a number of serious threats to our environment. We worry about climate change and how rising temperatures and sea levels may impact all life forms. Also on the global level we know that nearly a billion people suffer from malnutrition. In the upper Midwest we hear about the dangerous levels of nitrates in freshwater sources caused in part by modern methods of agriculture. These are illustrations that as a human community we are not doing the best possible job of caring for what God has created. With the knowledge we possess today, especially in the various branches of science, there is little justification for not rectifying these serious problems.

We might benefit from connecting with one or more organizations addressing these and many other issues. Lending our support to such organized efforts can be an effective way to exercise our "dominion over" or stewardship of the world that God has placed in our care. Such practical and direct involvement may help us as well to understand more clearly what the problem is and how we may be contributing to it. Finally, this activity may help us see God's presence and purpose in creation—a sure step toward developing and strengthening our relationship with this loving God who trusts us to look after his beautiful world.

*And How about Those Squirrels and Chipmunks?*

The second creation story tells us that we are created much like the other beings that inhabit the earth. We are made from the same dust of the earth as are the other animals, the birds and the fish. Our life on earth is shared with all of them as we are part of this same created order. And yet, Genesis 1—the first creation story—calls us to look after and to care for all other creatures. What does this mean today?

Surely this responsibility suggests that we act with kindness toward other living things, and, at the very least, that we not cause undue harm or hurt to any other creatures that God has placed upon this earth. This does not forbid the use of animals in ways that serve human needs, including raising animals for food. But it does mean that we do so in humane ways and with a grateful awareness that God has provided us what we need to live a reasonably comfortable life.

Squirrels and chipmunks, cows and chickens, walleye and pheasants—all of them add to the beauty of God's creation. None of them should be treated in ways that cause stress and suffering. To do so is to dishonor their Creator. A useful action flowing from this stance would be to look at one or more organizations dedicated to the humane treatment of all creatures, whether in pet stores, poultry facilities, or large-scale livestock confinements. Perhaps involvement in such activities might lead us to appreciate even more God's call to us to be stewards of his creation.

## Notes

1. *Didache* 4.8, in *The Apostolic Fathers*, trans. Francis X. Glimm, Joseph M.-F. Marique, and Gerald G. Walsh, The Fathers of the Church: A New Translation 1 (Washington, DC: Catholic University of America Press, 1947), 174.

2. Irenaeus of Lyons, *Against the Heresies* 2.1.1, in *St. Irenaeus of Lyons: Against the Heresies*, vol. 2, trans. Dominic J. Unger, Ancient Christian Writers 65 (Mahwah, NJ: Paulist, 2012), 17.

3. Gregory of Nazianzus, *Oration 38: On the Theophany* 11, qtd. in Brian E. Daley, *Gregory of Nazianzus*, The Early Church Fathers (New York: Routledge, 2006), 122.

# 2

# Caring for Ourselves and God's People

Then the king will say to those at his right hand, "Come, you that are blessed by my Father, inherit the kingdom prepared for you from the foundation of the world; for I was hungry and you gave me food."

—Matthew 25:34-35

If stewardship is about caring for God's creation, it is also about taking care of ourselves and looking after God's people. All of us are part of God's beautiful creation. Each of us deserves the love, protection, and care that stewardship implies. This part of creation that the Scriptures declare to be made in the likeness of God is worthy of all the nurturing and support that the Creator asks us to give. This approach to stewardship begins by treating ourselves with respect and appreciating the many gifts and talents that reside in us. It reaches maturity in our unselfish concern for the well-being of all God's people, especially those persons who struggle through life with the barest of necessities.

## Taking Care of Ourselves

The first responsibility of stewardship is to keep ourselves in a position where we are able to enjoy our lives and live them to the fullest, always striving to pursue healthy lifestyles marked by physical, social, and spiritual well-being. If we are able to do this, then we are likely to appreciate the beautiful world around us, and to celebrate the people in our lives who play so important a role in our efforts to live well. This approach to life, this commitment to living sound and healthy lifestyles, provides stability as we move from day to day as well as an openness to unexpected developments and an excitement about new and unforeseen directions our lives may take. It is a posture of gratitude for what we have and humble acceptance of the challenges and opportunities God may send in our direction.

Taking care of ourselves requires that we see our lives unfolding within the context of one or more communities. These communities allow us to draw guidance from the wisdom and love of so many other people in our lives, and in turn offer support to persons whose lives we share in these communities. It is in this dynamic of communal giving and receiving that we accept the responsibility of caring for ourselves and enjoy the blessings that accompany living and working with others to achieve balanced living.

Taking care of ourselves—striving to live this healthy lifestyle—is our first and unending movement to become the people whom God has called us to be. A never-ending challenge, this effort unfolds through our entire life. Obviously this journey takes many turns and encounters numerous obstacles, some of our own making. How well we adjust and are able to correct our direction may depend upon that foundation—the healthy lifestyle—we have been building. That in turn provides comfort and encouragement as we struggle to follow the road we know we need to take, even when tempted by alluring side streets.

If we ever doubt the importance of caring for ourselves, including our physical bodies, it might be helpful to read again what St. Paul says about treating and using our bodies properly:

> Do you not know that you are God's temple and that God's Spirit dwells in you? If anyone destroys God's temple, God will destroy that person. For God's temple is holy, and you are that temple. (1 Cor 3:16-17)

Giving reasonable attention to keeping our bodies in a sound state can be a step toward having social, psychological, and spiritual well-being.

In his discussion of sexual offenses in chapter 6, Paul again says that our bodies are temples of the Holy Spirit, adding, "and that you are not your own" (v. 19). Here we have a reminder that our bodies and our lives belong to God and for that reason especially we must never abuse or misuse our bodies in any way. Rather, we should strive to be healthy and not neglect our physical needs, even as we recognize that unexpected and unavoidable illness may be with us at any time.

This reminder from St. Paul that we are temples of the Holy Spirit and that our bodies "are not [our] own" is not only a warning to avoid sins of the flesh. It also serves as a call to treat our bodies as the God-given wonders they are. Striving to respect our bodies and keeping them healthy is a fundamental part of caring for ourselves. It maintains the possibility as well that we, with our bodies, become a medium through which the Holy Spirit is present and active in the world. In Psalm 104 we read that the Spirit of God shall "renew the face of the ground [earth]" (v. 30). The Spirit of God works through all of us. Each of us has a role to play in that holy endeavor of renewing the face of the earth. But we can carry out this task only if we first care for ourselves.

## Recognizing Our Gifts

Our part in caring for God's people begins with a recognition and acceptance of our own gifts and talents. We do so not in a boastful way that credits everything to ourselves, but from a posture of humbly acknowledging that God has put a lot in us and we need to make it flourish.

Saint Paul challenged the Corinthians on this point—to recognize the source of their talents, resources, and accomplishments:

> What do you have that you did not receive? And if you received it, why do you boast as if it were not a gift? (1 Cor 4:7)

The New Testament repeatedly tells us that we enjoy endless blessings from God. Some of these come in the form of particular talents and gifts. Each of us can point to special abilities we possess as well as the resources that permit us to pursue goals and projects for which we carry great passion. Too often we forget that these talents, these capacities to accomplish great things, are not of our own making, but are received. Much of who we are and what we are able to accomplish is because of what we have received from our parents and family lineage, or from the schools we have attended, or the communities in which we lived. Ultimately it is because of what we received from God mediated through so many people in our lives.

There may be times when we are quite satisfied with what we have done, times when others around us praise us for one accomplishment or another. Sometimes a letter to the editor in a local newspaper criticizes certain groups or individuals for not doing well with their lives, while citing the writer's own accomplishments as proof that persons who don't complete high school or people on public assistance could do better. Especially at these moments we need to remember who gave us the skills, abilities, desires, and ambition to do well. Who made it possible for us to achieve?

These talents and gifts are given for a purpose. They provide the way and the means for us to move through life reflecting at every moment the compassion and mercy God bestows on every one of us. That reflection of God's love begins with caring for ourselves and for all God's people. That is a lifelong task and for that reason we must nurture and develop these abilities every day of our lives.

In his 1967 encyclical, On the Development of Peoples, Pope Paul VI developed this point:

> In the design of God, every man is called upon to develop and fulfill himself, for every life is a vocation. At birth, everyone is granted, in germ, a set of aptitudes and qualities for him to bring to fruition. Their coming to maturity, which will be the result of education received from the environment and personal efforts,

will allow each man to direct himself toward the destiny intended for him by his Creator. (15)

Recognizing, developing, and using the gifts we have enjoyed since birth is a way of "direct[ing] [ourselves] toward the destiny" that God has in mind for us.

How often we hear people say they wish they could know what God wants them to become. Why doesn't God make it clearer what we should do with our lives? In one sense God does make this clear, or at least God provides fairly strong hints about where we should go with our lives. Those indications are found in the gifts and skills, the interests and passions that we receive from our Creator. Paying attention to these, developing them, using them throughout our lives may offer the best assurance that we are following God's calling, that we accept the fact that—as Paul VI wrote—our life is a vocation.

In the language of St. Paul these "gifts . . . of God are irrevocable" (Rom 11:29). They are intimately connected to our life's vocation. Each of us enjoys a sacred dignity. Each of us is created by God, redeemed by Christ, and called to communion with God. This is never lost; God never takes this back. Nor does God recall the particular talents he places within us. These are ours for life and they are an important part of living out our vocation, of becoming the fully human and morally responsible creatures God desires us to be.

God's gifts to us are something to which we must respond. To live as persons who have been redeemed and called to everlasting happiness with God is not something we do without effort. To figure out what this means in the context of our ordinary daily lives is a challenge. Equally important, to believe in an eternal destiny for ourselves and for all people necessarily changes the way we live today.

One thing that should not change is our commitment to utilize to the fullest the resources with which we have been endowed. Throughout our lives there are many ways and many occasions where we both use and continue to develop those resources, those particular talents and gifts that help to define each of us. One of the most common places for this to happen is in our job or career.

The earliest of Catholic social encyclicals takes up this idea when it addresses the topic of human work (On the Condition of Labor, Pope Leo XIII, 1891). It speaks of work as both necessary and personal. Work is necessary because this is how most of us make our living, working at regular jobs so that we have the income needed for a reasonably decent living. Our jobs provide us with the necessities we require for life—food, some kind of housing, basic clothing, access to health care services, education.

But work, according to Catholic social teaching, is also personal. The work we do in our jobs while earning a living is one place where we put to use whatever talents God has given us. It is, at the same time, one of the places and one of the activities in our lives where we continue to develop these skills.

This is the personal side of work. It is the daily practice of putting to use whatever gifts we have, and in doing so we realize our vocation, our calling from God. Even when we change jobs or careers this holds true. Such changes may occur through necessity as when we lose our job and need to find another one. But we sometimes change careers because we are seeking something more challenging, something that better utilizes our particular skill sets—a job that puts us into a stronger position to grow the talents God has given us.

When church teachings speak of the dignity of work, they are referring to the person doing the work. The human person—the worker—is the reference point for appreciating the value of any kind of work. Pope John Paul II wrote in 1981 that "the basis for determining the value of human work is not primarily the kind of work being done, but the fact that the one who is doing it is a person" (On Human Work 6). From that perspective any job has value and dignity because the working person possesses the dignity of one created in the image of God. Through this labor we earn our daily bread and we become more fully developed human persons.

Our work also is a way in which we contribute to the larger community, to the common good. As we earn our income—as farmers, nurses, factory workers, teachers, delivery persons—we help to provide goods or services that are needed by society. This too is a way to appreciate the value of the gifts we have received and the importance of using them. They are given to meet our own needs and those of the larger community as well. Pope Leo XIII emphasized this point: "Thus to sum up what has been said: whoever has received from the divine bounty a larger share of blessings, whether these be external and corporal or gifts of mind, has received them for the purpose of using them for perfecting his own nature, and, at the same time, that he may employ them, as the minister of God's providence, for the benefit of others" (On the Condition of Labor 19). Subsequent documents in the Catholic social teaching tradition will clarify and expand this point. It is not only those who have received "a larger share of blessings" but every one of us who must use whatever gifts we have to benefit others and to build up the community.

## Taking Care of God's People

Biblical stewardship directs us to use our gifts for the larger community. Jesus' command that we love one another has very practical overtones. It means that we demonstrate this love in concrete acts of service to one another. It means responding to our neighbor according to his or her needs and our capacity to help. It especially means using what resources we possess to assist those persons who are poor, vulnerable, or marginalized in any way. This was a constant reminder from the Hebrew prophets to the people of Israel—if you wish to be in right relationship with God, take care of the widows, the orphans, and the strangers.

Christians in the earliest postbiblical period understood well this expectation that they were to share their resources. The first-century *Didache* presents this in clear and direct language: "Give to everyone who asks, and ask nothing in return; for the Father wishes that a share of his own gifts be given to all.[1] Again the reminder, what we possess is not ours but rather the Father's "gracious bounty." We are simply instruments for making sure this bounty is shared among those who ask for help. A century later the *Letter to Diognetus* developed this teaching:

> There is no real happiness in getting the better of your neighbors, in wanting to have more than weaker men, in being rich and able to order your inferiors about. It is not in such ways that a man can be an imitator of God, for these things are no part of His greatness. On the other hand, any man can be an imitator of God, if he takes on his own shoulders the burden of his neighbors, if he chooses to use his advantage to help another who is underprivileged, if he takes what he has received from God and gives it to those who are in need—for such a man becomes God to those who are helped.[2]

To shoulder our neighbor's burden, to use our talents and resources to make life just a bit easier for another person or group of individuals: this is living the Gospel mandate to love our neighbor. Through such benevolent behavior we in some way become imitators of God.

We are members of various communities and all of them function because of the contributions of many members. The earliest Christian communities carried out Christ's ministry in this way—utilizing the many different gifts of the Spirit present among the members for building up the body (Rom 12:6). They encouraged one another to be generous to members of other Christian communities, following the example of St. Paul to collect money for the brethren suffering in distant lands.

Already during the patristic period leaders of the Christian communities at times encouraged members to assist people who did not share their faith. During a third-century plague in North Africa the bishop of Carthage, Cyprian, exhorted his Christians to give generously to persons stricken by the plague, whether they were Christians or pagans (On Works and Almsgiving 5). Many centuries later, modern Catholic social teachings repeatedly call on Christians to care for God's people through acts of charity and justice, acts that should be carried out on behalf of anyone in need regardless of religious affiliation. That teaching is modeled in the work of the Catholic Campaign for Human Development, which annually grants millions of dollars to self-help, social change projects in communities in poverty throughout the United States, and once again religious identity is not a factor in determining where grants should be allocated.

As individuals within the Christian community, each of us has something to give in support of our communities or to lift up those who are hurting. No one should ever doubt that he or she can be a positive force. The First Letter of Peter tells us that "whoever serves must do so with the strength that God supplies, so that God may be glorified in all things through Jesus Christ" (1 Pet 4:11). This is comforting assurance that every one of us has something to lend to the service of others and to the building of the community. We need not worry about having to do more than we are able, about meeting others' expectations to perform beyond our capacity. God has granted us particular gifts to help make the community work, and the strength to use them well—especially in the service of others—and, as 1 Peter notes, our humble act of serving others gives glory to God.

We can point to various biblical texts that call us to serve our neighbor. We recall Jesus' many examples of how we should use our gifts in the service of God's people. Many of his signs that the reign of God had come near took the form of sometimes simple, sometimes powerful acts of mercy and compassion on behalf of persons with practical needs—healing the sick, feeding the multitudes, forgiving the sinner, raising the dead. Among the New Testament texts, perhaps none is clearer on the connection between caring for God's people and participating in the reign of God than the parable of the Last Judgment:

> Then the king will say to those at his right hand,
> "Come, you that are blessed by my Father, inherit the
> kingdom prepared for you from the foundation of the
> world; for I was hungry and you gave me food, I was
> thirsty and you gave me something to drink, I was a
> stranger and you welcomed me, I was naked and you
> gave me clothing, I was sick and you took care of me,
> I was in prison and you visited me." (Matt 25:34-36)

In this parable we find a stunning connection made between
our entry into eternal happiness and the way we conduct our
lives here on earth. More specifically, entry into the kingdom is
dependent upon how we treat our neighbors on a daily basis,
especially that neighbor with great needs. Our talents, gifts,
and resources must be used to feed the hungry, give drink to
the thirsty, welcome the stranger, clothe the naked, care for the
sick, visit those in prison. Failure to act in this way, a refusal
to use our gifts and resources in this manner, invites denial
of entry into the kingdom:

> Then he will say to those on his left hand, "You that
> are accursed, depart from me into the eternal fire pre-
> pared for the devil and his angels; for I was hungry
> and you gave me no food, I was thirsty and you gave
> me nothing to drink . . ." (Matt 25:41-42)

It seems difficult not to recognize that our enjoyment of
eternal happiness has something to do with how we do or do
not serve the poorest among us. The faith we claim to have in
Jesus Christ must show itself in such acts. Jesus' command to
love our neighbor must prove itself in our concrete response
to the needs of our neighbors who are most marginalized. To
be a disciple of Jesus Christ means to act as he did.

We might keep in mind as well that when Jesus asks us
to love and serve our neighbor in need, it does not matter
whether we are able to see Christ in such persons. The message in the parable of the Last Judgment is quite simple: do

it! As the king in this story said to the surprised people on the right, as long as you did it to one of the least of my sisters and brothers, you did it to me. The Second Vatican Council reminds us, with reference to this parable, that caring for God's people extends to a broad range of persons in need:

> Today, there is an inescapable duty to make ourselves the neighbor of every individual, without exception, and to take positive steps to help a neighbor whom we encounter, whether that neighbor be an elderly person abandoned by everyone, a foreign worker who suffers the injustice of being despised, a refugee, an illegitimate child wrongly suffering for a sin of which the child is innocent, or a starving human being who awakens our conscience by calling to mind the words of Christ: "As you did it to one of the least of these my brothers or sisters, you did it to me" (Mt 25:40). (Pastoral Constitution on the Church in the Modern World 27)

The early Christian writers understood well this connection between entry into the kingdom and serving God's people, especially those who live on the fringes of society. In the fourth century Gregory of Nyssa wrote,

> The poor are the treasurers of the good things that we look for, the keepers of the gates of the kingdom, opening them to the merciful and shutting them on the harsh and uncharitable. They are the strongest of accusers, the best of defenders—not that they accuse or defend in words, but that the Lord beholds what is done toward them, and every deed cries louder than a herald to him who searches all hearts.[3]

Gregory reminds us that service to God's people must take the form of actions, not just words or pious platitudes intended to demonstrate our faith. Practical gestures and meaningful forms of loving assistance must characterize the life of any person who claims to be a follower of Jesus Christ. To fail in this is to stand before God accused by those we chose not to help.

Continuing this theme, St. John Chrysostom, also in the fourth century, asked, "Don't you realize that, as the poor man withdraws silently, sighing and in tears, you actually thrust a sword into yourself, that it is you who received the more serious wound?"[4] In another homily on Matthew's gospel, John Chrysostom preached on caring for Christ's body:

> Do you really wish to pay homage to Christ's body? Then do not neglect him when he is naked. At the same time that you honor him here (in church) with hangings made of silk, do not ignore him outside when he perishes from cold and nakedness. For the one who said, "This is my body" . . . also said, "When I was hungry you gave me nothing to eat."[5]

For Chrysostom, our sister and brother in distress is more truly God's temple than any church building. Recognizing Christ's body in the sacramental bread and wine is a given in Catholic liturgical practice. As important as that liturgical practice, however, is recognizing Christ's body in the hungry and homeless people of our world. Taking care of God's people in this way, and responding to anyone who is hurting in any way, is essential for our journey to God. It is a form of stewardship we overlook at our own risk.

## ✍ Getting Practical

### Pursuing a Healthy, Gifted, and Caring Lifestyle

Our religious and theological resources encourage us to live healthy lives, to enjoy our lives, and to make life better for others. This is a form of stewardship because it commits us to caring for something that belongs to God. That something includes our own lives and the lives of God's people anywhere.

*Staying Healthy—in Every Way*

An elderly aunt recovering from a serious illness once told me, don't wait until you are sick before you begin to pray. It is easier to pray, she said, when you have a healthy body and mind. This seems like sound advice: to work on our prayer life early and always, and not wait until serious problems develop in our lives. Aunt Fran's advice was to let prayer be a regular part of our lives and let it shape who we are and who we are becoming. The same can be said for other areas of our lives—our physical health, mental and intellectual stimulation, emotional well-being. These, too, we need to be working on, always.

The area of prayer, however, can be a particular challenge. We know it is important and most of us recognize that if we are to benefit from a healthy prayer life, then we need to plan when, where, and how we will pray, and we need to commit ourselves to this. A resource that lends itself well to this effort is the beautiful daily prayer periodical *Give Us This Day* available from Liturgical Press. Each day offers Scripture readings, reflections, morning and evening prayers, and a writing on the saint or feast commemorated that day. Busy people can use as little or as much of each day's offerings as they are able. Liturgically oriented, this is a solid resource that helps us connect personal prayer with the public prayer of the church and, most important, to pray daily.

*Enjoying and Using Our Gifts*

The psalms wonder at the magnificence of God's creation and so should we. But creation includes ourselves: the wonderful bodies we have been given, the particular interests that influence where we go and what we become, and the many gifts needed to pursue these interests. Part of living a healthy lifestyle is knowing ourselves, acknowledging and celebrating the many characteristics that make us who we are—our strengths and weaknesses, our hopes and fears, our passions and aversions.

A practice that can benefit all of us is to listen carefully when family, friends, classmates, or coworkers speak of the good qualities and positive attributes they see in us, when they acknowledge the talents we have. We may be adept at hearing criticisms directed our way because we somehow expect that and because we don't always appreciate the good we represent. But other people in our lives do appreciate and enjoy pointing out what they like about us. We need to hear this as part of our being able to recognize and utilize the gifts God has given us. And, we need to do the same for other people, especially teenagers and young adults who are trying to set their life's course. They too can use help in seeing in themselves the wonderful gifts and blessings from their God.

### Caring for Others as Part of Our Lifestyle

The Christian must respond to the needs of others. The Scriptures, the early Christian writers, and modern Catholic social teachings present this as an absolute requirement of living the Christian life. Caring for God's people must be a daily practice, not a once-a-year occurrence, for example, of serving meals to the homeless in a church basement on Thanksgiving Day or an occasional check sent to aid people living on the other side of the planet. Caring for others—within or outside our families—should happen on a daily basis.

A way to help us grow in this sense of stewardship might be to develop the habit of responding to people around us, whatever their needs. Let this become our way of living—through often small gestures and acts to make the day a bit better for a person with whom we work or study or pass on the street. The more we do this, the more habitual it becomes on a daily basis, the more likely we are to respond to another person's greater needs when these are evident to us. This also moves us further in the direction of caring for ourselves and for God's people. It is helping us to appreciate that when we care for God's people, we are caring for ourselves.

# Notes

1. *Didache* 1.5, in *The Apostolic Fathers*, trans. Francis X. Glimm, Joseph M.-F. Marique, and Gerald G. Walsh, The Fathers of the Church: A New Translation 1 (Washington, DC: Catholic University of America Press, 1947), 172.

2. *Letter to Diognetus* 10, in *The Apostolic Fathers*, 366.

3. Gregory of Nyssa, *On the Love of the Poor*, in Peter C. Phan, *Social Thought*, Message of the Fathers of the Church 20 (Wilmington, DE: Michael Glazier, 1984), 132.

4. John Chrysostom, Homily 35 on Matthew, quoted in William J. Walsh and John P. Langan, "Patristic Social Consciousness—The Church and the Poor," *The Faith That Does Justice: Examining the Christian Sources for Social Change*, ed. John C. Haughey, Woodstock Studies 2 (New York: Paulist, 1977), 118.

5. Ibid., 131.

# 3

# Justice and Relationships

But let justice roll down like waters,
and righteousness like an ever-flowing stream.

—Amos 5:24

Stewardship is about caring for creation. It is about appreciating and fully using the gifts God has given us—using them for ourselves and for others. Stewardship also is a matter of justice.

Using our resources to benefit others is not an optional activity for a Christian. It is not simply a nice thing to do or an action found on a list of what is recommended for a life of decency. Sharing God's gifts with others has the character of an obligation that stems from who we are and what our standing with God requires. Such expected behavior, in fact, defines what it means to be in relationship with God and with our neighbor. Again, it is a matter of justice.

The word "justice" carries many meanings depending upon the setting and who is using the word. To connect justice with stewardship is to suggest that the practice of stewardship is a requirement for one who strives to live the Christian faith. To appreciate why this is so it will be helpful to explore how the Scriptures, the early Christian writers, and Catholic social teachings speak both about justice and about how we are to use our gifts.

**Justice as Faithfulness**

The Scriptures present us with a rich appreciation of justice that flows out of relationships. The biblical sense of justice involves living according to the expectations of our relationships, particularly the one we have with God. For the people of Israel the covenant they entered into with Yahweh on Mount Sinai carried a number of expectations. Striving to live faithfully to those demands was the mark of a person or community seeking to live justly. These requirements of the covenant moved in two directions.

The God of Abraham, Isaac, and Jacob promised that he would be the God of this people fleeing captivity in Egypt. He would be with them and protect them always. And, he would lead them into a good land. For their part the people of Israel would honor and worship this God and only this God. They would put their trust in him and they would not seek the protection of other nations. They would obey Yahweh's commands and they would care for one another. "I will be your God and you will be my people." The biblical sense of justice is rooted in the recognition that relationships carry certain expectations or demands. This is as true for a marital relationship or a parent-child relationship as it is for our relationship with our God. This is not a difficult concept, and it is one we accept in our lives today as did the people of the Bible in their time. Further, it shows us the most basic aspect of living justly—that is, being faithful. Without such faithfulness there can be no life-giving relationship.

We easily recognize that when two people enter into a marriage they make commitments to each other. Each partner rightfully expects to live out these commitments, to be faithful to the promises made, to the expectations that now flow from their union. Justice is about striving to meet these expectations. Although our relationship with God cannot be equated with marriage or any other human relationship, it does offer points of contact for illustrating the biblical sense of justice. Nor should we overlook how often the biblical writers use the marriage metaphor to explain Israel's standing with God.

From a scriptural perspective, being in good standing with
God necessarily includes being in good standing with our
neighbors. It means we hold together the two great commandments that Jesus gave us:

> "You shall love the Lord your God with all your heart,
> and with all your soul, and with all your mind." . . .
> "You shall love your neighbor as yourself." On these
> two commandments hang all the law and the prophets.
> (Matt 22:37-40)

Love of God and love of neighbor cannot be separated, and
within that commandment is a particular summons to care
for the neighbor with needs greater than our own. This biblical sense of justice, this call to stewardship in the use of our
gifts, directs us in a special way to look out for those among
us who are poor and vulnerable.

The prophets of the Hebrew Scriptures often presented this
obligation to the people of Israel, sometimes in fairly judgmen-
tal language. It was their unpleasant—and unrequested—task
to point out to the people that they were not living up to the
demands of their agreement with God, that their covenant
with Yahweh was broken. Among the signs the prophets cited
as evidence that the people were not carrying out the expectations of this covenantal relationship was their neglect of the
poor among them.

Jeremiah provides an illustration. He lays out the case that
the people are not living in faithfulness to the demands of
their covenant with God. Then he succinctly tells them what
a return to good standing with their God requires of them:

> For if you truly amend your ways and your doings,
> if you truly act justly one with another, if you do not
> oppress the alien, the orphan, and the widow, or shed
> innocent blood in this place, and if you do not go after
> other gods to your own hurt, then I will dwell with
> you in this place, in the land that I gave of old to your
> ancestors forever and ever. (Jer 7:5-7)

Justice requires that we honor and fulfill the demands or expectations that come with our many relationships. For the Hebrew people their primary one was with their God, and this was a God who demonstrated a special love for people who were marginalized. They once were that marginalized people living as slaves in Egypt, and their God intervened to lead them out of this servitude and into the land promised to their forefathers. Their response—their living faithfully with this God according to the terms of the covenant—requires that they likewise show compassion to the marginalized of any age. They must use their resources as a community and their individual gifts to assist the widows, the orphans, and the strangers.

This biblical understanding of justice was a topic of reflection within Christian communities during the second, third, and fourth centuries. Early Christian writers addressed the subject within the context of their own communities, focusing especially on how disciples of Jesus Christ should use their resources. How should a Christian respond to her neighbor in need? How must a follower of Christ regard riches? The emphasis in these discussions was on how members of the Christian community should use their material possessions as well as their personal gifts and talents, and what attitude should guide their choices.

A common theme among a number of these writers on the topic of proper use of our gifts was that of gratitude. The *Letter to Diognetus*, for example, develops the point that we must be thankful for all that God has done for us and for all the gifts he has bestowed on each of us. An appropriate way to express this gratitude is to imitate God by loving our sisters and brothers—to use these gifts we have received from God to benefit those around us. Repeating this thought in the third century, St. Cyprian wrote that sharing what we have with the poor makes us imitators of God. Cyprian stresses the obligatory character of such actions when he writes, "For he will not be able to merit the mercy of God who himself has not been merciful, nor will gain any request from the divine love by his prayers, who has not been humane toward the prayer of the poor."[1] If we do not act with loving kindness toward our neighbor, we should not expect God to look favorably upon our petitions. The two are related—justice, expectations.

A statement by St. Ambrose of Milan in the fourth century reflects much of early Christian thinking on how we should use our gifts, including monetary wealth. Writing on the matter of almsgiving, Ambrose stated, "It is not anything of yours that you are bestowing on the poor; rather, you are giving back something of his."[2] This is the biblical theme that all creation belongs to God and everything within creation is intended by God to meet the needs of all people. The early Christian writers articulated this in terms of the universal purpose of the goods of creation.

Saint John Chrysostom used this principle in chiding his listeners as he preached on the gospel figure of Lazarus: "Do not say 'I am using what belongs to me.' You are using what belongs to others in common as the sun, air, earth and all the rest."[3] Ambrose also wrote on this principle of the universal purpose of the goods of creation:

> God has ordered all things to be produced so that there should be food in common to all, and that the earth should be a common possession for all. Nature, therefore, has produced a common right for all, but greed has made it a right for a few.[4]

For Christians this means that whatever gifts we possess or whatever we own certainly may be used to meet our own needs and the needs of family members and others dependent upon us. It also means that we are to use our resources to satisfy the needs of the larger community, especially those among us who might not be doing too well.

To glance ahead many hundreds of years, this teaching of the earliest Christian theologians provided the grounds for St. Thomas Aquinas to assert in the thirteenth century that a person in extreme need has the right to take from the riches of others—and, this is not stealing (*Summa Theologiae* II-II, q. 66, a. 7). The Second Vatican Council repeated this teaching in 1965 with the added footnote, "In extreme necessity all goods are common, that is, they are to be shared" (Church in the Modern World 69, n. 11).

The biblical understanding of justice suggests that our relationship with God carries certain expectations regarding how we live. To live justly requires us to fulfill those demands, including that of caring for our brothers and sisters. The quality of our standing with God is linked to how we treat our neighbor. The early Christian theologians were clear on the point that everything God provided in creation is intended to meet the needs of everyone. That includes our own material possessions and the many gifts that God has placed within us. That too is a necessary form of stewardship; it is a matter of justice.

### Worship and Living Justly

For the people of Israel and for us today, this way of living—this willingness to share our gifts and resources with others—is a necessary dimension of our response to God's love. This form of stewardship is as important as our acts of worship. Most of us at some level recognize the importance of worship in which we adore, praise, and glorify God our Creator and Savior. But we don't always appreciate how our acts of worship must be validated in daily actions toward our neighbor. The prophets in the Hebrew Scriptures drew this connection between worshiping God and living justly:

> I hate, I despise your festivals,
>     and I take no delight in your solemn assemblies.
> Even though you offer me your burnt offerings
>         and grain offerings,
>     I will not accept them;
> and the offerings of well-being of your fatted animals
>     I will not look upon.
> Take away from me the noise of your songs;
>     I will not listen to the melody of your harps.

> But let justice roll down like waters,
>> and righteousness like an ever-flowing stream.
>>   (Amos 5:21-24)

It is unlikely that Amos was condemning worship outright. Rather, the problem here is worship that does not lead to actions and lifestyles marked by a deep awareness of our responsibilities for one another—such worship is not acceptable or pleasing to God.

Isaiah presents an even clearer connection between acts of piety and our response, or failure to respond, to sisters and brothers in need. Chapter 58 relates how the people are complaining that they fast so diligently but God does not seem to notice. Through the words of the prophet God responds to their complaint by pointing out that instead of their publicity-seeking approach to fasting, he expects something else:

> Is not this the fast that I choose:
>> to loose the bonds of injustice,
>> to undo the thongs of the yoke . . .
> Is it not to share your bread with the hungry,
>> and bring the homeless poor into your house;
> when you see the naked, to cover them . . . ?
>   (Isa 58:6-7)

Fasting provides a helpful way to see the connection between ritual acts of piety and our practical willingness to use our gifts in ways that benefit others. Fasting says something about being stewards of our gifts so that we may connect with God as well as our neighbor. Denying ourselves some amount of food can be a way for us to unite with those who suffer. On a more practical level it can provide us the opportunity to share with those who are always hungry.

Early Christian writers also valued the practice of fasting as a way of fulfilling the expectations that come with our relationship to God and to neighbor, as a way of living justly. In the second century the Shepherd of Hermas laid out quite specific instructions on how fasting benefits our neighbors who may be hurting:

> On the day of your fast do not taste anything except
> bread and water. Compute the total expense for the
> food you would have eaten on the day on which you
> intended to keep a fast and give it to a widow, an or-
> phan, or someone in need.[5]

There is nothing abstract about these instructions. Fasting,
whatever else it may accomplish, should result in marginalized persons receiving monetary assistance.

Two hundred years later St. Augustine played with an Epi-
curean maxim and connected fasting with a poor person being
able to eat:

> Let no one say, "Let us eat and drink for tomorrow
> we die," but rather . . . "Let us fast and pray, for to-
> morrow we die." I add . . . a third step . . . that as a
> result of your fast the poor man's hunger be satisfied;
> and, should you be unable to fast, that you give him
> more to eat.[6]

Fasting provided an opportunity to do what is expected by a
person who loves God and God's people. Fasting may help us
draw closer to God through self-denial and it may be good for
our health, but it also brings comfort and aid to our sisters
and brothers. To fast and still neglect people who are poor is
a missed opportunity, and it distorts what fasting should be.

Many years ago as a Peace Corps Volunteer living in a Mus-
lim community, I observed this beautiful practice of connecting fasting and caring for one's neighbor. During the holy time
of Ramadan we observed the complete fast—no food or water
between the rising and setting of the sun. These were long and
challenging days and I learned the benefits of serious fasting.
But the greater lesson I learned was how a people committed to religiously motivated fasting would then intensify their
efforts to assist the poor in their midst. During my two years
in this small Turkish town I was repeatedly impressed by the
generosity of this people who had so little but were willing to
share with those who had even less, especially during the fast.

Faithfulness to God, living out the expectations of our relationship with God, involves more than prayer and fasting. Liturgy as public worship of God is vitally important to our life as a faith community; it is the source of our life in the church. But if it doesn't lead to acts of mercy, service, and justice, then we need to ask, What are we doing in worship?

In his encyclical God Is Love (2005), Pope Benedict XVI reflected this point: "A Eucharist which does not pass over into the concrete practice of love is intrinsically fragmented" (14). Our public worship, our liturgy, must form us and empower us to respond to the needs of others. This is not a new twenty-first-century addition to Christian theology. The Letter of James made this same point with reference to religion more generally:

> Religion that is pure and undefiled before God, the Father, is this: to care for orphans and widows in their distress, and to keep oneself unstained by the world. (1:27)

Stewardship of God's resources, especially those to which we are connected in any way, means using them to feed the hungry, to shelter the homeless, to clothe the naked. It means to do as Jesus called us to do in Matthew 25.

### Justice as Social Change

All of us must respond to God's love and God's call, and this we do in many different ways. Perhaps the most important manner in which each of us responds to God is by striving to grow as mature moral persons. Part of this is living responsibly—taking responsibility—for our lives, for those dependent upon us, and for the larger community. In this way we utilize our talents and resources not only for our personal advancement but also for persons beyond our immediate family and circle of friends. This is what Catholic social teaching means when it speaks of everyone's obligation to contribute to the common good. In making such contributions we know that

we enrich ourselves even as we help to create a social environment in which everyone may flourish.

For some among us that task and that responsibility are not
easily realized. The obligation that each of us has to respond
to God's love by caring for ourselves and others can prove
difficult. Living conditions, the social context within which we
carry on our lives, can make it very difficult for some persons
and some groups to realize this fundamental dimension of
human dignity. The Second Vatican Council noted how ad-
verse living conditions can add to the challenge of pursuing
a morally responsible life:

> But this sense of responsibility will not be achieved un-
> less people are so circumstanced that they are aware
> of their dignity and are capable of responding to their
> calling in the service of God and of humanity. For
> freedom is often crippled by extreme destitution, just
> as it can wither in an ivory-tower isolation brought on
> by overindulgence in the good things of life. (Church
> in the Modern World 31)

Poverty, deprivation, and oppression can have the same negative effects on a person as an all-consuming passion for wealth
or excessive indulgence in the material comforts of life. Both
extremes—poverty and overindulgence—diminish a person's
capacity for living a full human life, a life characterized by
care for others and a willingness to use our resources to help
build the larger community. This is a life in which a person is
committed to growth in every possible way.

Over the past decades millions of persons have left their
home countries in search of better employment in the United
States. Some of them—perhaps as many as eleven million—
have entered this country without legal documentation, and
as a result they live every day in fear of being discovered and
deported. For some this can mean separation from family
members. This is not the kind of living environment that allows
people to become "aware of their dignity" and to respond to
"their calling in the service of God and of humanity."

Likewise, a life marked by the effects of homelessness and hunger, or tyranny and persecution—like a life lost in a blinding pursuit of wealth and consumerism—is not a life that easily reflects the ideals of human moral development. Nor are persons struggling with such a life likely to enjoy the luxury of appreciating the many blessings and gifts they have received from their Creator. Still less should we expect them, in the midst of a survival mode, to place their resources at the service of others.

For this reason in the Christian churches we speak so much of the need to change whatever conditions keep people from social and moral development, from responding to God's love and becoming the people God calls us to be. For this reason we speak of social justice.

Social justice is one of the most important but neglected dimensions of "loving our neighbor as ourselves." If our love of God and our love of neighbor are connected, then we need to be clear on what love of neighbor entails. In other words, we must appreciate the connection between love and justice, between responding to our neighbor's immediate needs and striving to bring about changes so that these needs do not linger on indefinitely.

As noted in the previous chapter, the parable of the Last Judgment makes it clear that our entry into the kingdom of God is dependent upon our responding to the neighbor in need, whether that be a person who is hungry or thirsty or naked or sick or in jail. To love our neighbor as ourselves, as Jesus commanded, means that we not only provide that food or water when we see the need. To love our neighbor also means we do what we can to make sure he or she is not hungry tomorrow, nor sick and without medical care. This latter action moves us into the area of social justice.

Still, this term is poorly understood within many Catholic parishes. For many people the term conjures up radical actions that are best avoided. Parish social ministry efforts often do not go beyond direct service projects because parish leaders fear the change actions that social justice requires. Few terms are as widely misunderstood in the Catholic community as this two-word name of a ministry that is central to the mission of the church. Because social justice is likewise an integral part of stewardship, it is important that we understand what it means in the Catholic context and why a Christian—at least from a Catholic perspective—cannot ignore it.

In Catholic social teachings the term "social justice" first appears in the 1931 encyclical of Pope Pius XI, *Quadragesimo Anno*. There the Holy Father made the point that workers need to receive a wage "adequate to meet ordinary domestic needs," and he added,

> If in the present state of society this is not always feasible, social justice demands that reforms be introduced without delay which will guarantee every adult workingman just such a raise. (71)

From that time (1931) to the present, when Catholic social documents speak of social justice it is with reference to social changes that are needed so that individuals or groups have a better chance of living a responsible and dignified life. One of the clearest explanations of social justice is found in the 1986 pastoral letter of the United States Catholic bishops:

> Social justice implies that persons have an obligation to be active and productive participants in the life of society and that society has a duty to empower them to participate in this way. (Economic Justice for All 71)

Two critical points emerge from this statement of what social justice entails. The first is that every person must contribute to the larger community. All members of society must strive to carry out their duty and exercise their right to participate in the task of building healthy communities. This is part of our response to God's love and to God's call. Our obligations do not end with meeting our personal needs, nor even with helping to satisfy the needs of our family. We also must work for the good of the communities of which we are a part; we must become "active and productive participants in the life of society."

But, as already seen through teachings of the Second Vatican Council, people sometimes find themselves in living conditions so debased that they are unable to contribute to the common good. Worse, persons facing extreme poverty or struggling with inhumane political oppression often find it difficult to experience the kind of freedom and responsibility needed for moral development. When such living conditions exist, changes must be enacted, and that is where we turn to the second critical point in the bishops' statement about social justice.

Society must make it possible for everyone to participate, to contribute to the common good. People who lose their jobs during a recession and have to sleep in their cars because they can't afford house or apartment rents are quite naturally focused on getting through each day. When living conditions such as hunger and homelessness make it difficult for some to realize their dignity, to take responsibility for their lives and to contribute to the common good, then society needs to enact changes. These may be changes in the systems of health care or education; they may be changes in policies related to tax provisions or living wages; they may be changes leading to programs such as job training or access to affordable housing.

The purpose of social change is ultimately to empower individuals and groups living on the margins of life to become "active and productive participants in the life of society." The desired outcome in this effort is to create a society in which everyone can have what is needed for a dignified life and be positioned to realize his or her own responsibilities more fully.

That is why in Catholic moral teaching the term "social justice" always means change of a systemic or structural nature. Each of us as an individual needs to change, to undergo continual conversion. So also there is ongoing need for change on the communal or social level. There is, in other words, need for us as a society to continually evaluate our economic, social, political, and cultural systems and structures to make sure they are working for everyone—especially for those persons in society who may be poor or marginalized in any way. This is the kind of change that stands behind the term "social justice."

This also is a form of stewardship: using our abilities and resources to empower our brothers and sisters to use theirs. Social justice contains a recognition that every person enjoys a sacred dignity. It recognizes also that all persons possess gifts and talents for supporting themselves and for building up the people of God, for contributing to the common good. Social justice actions always aim to empower individuals or groups to move into positions that make it possible for them to put these God-given resources to good use.

Practicing stewardship means caring for creation as well as caring for ourselves and developing the gifts within us. It also means sharing these gifts and resources as a matter of justice. To develop, nurture, and maintain the friendship with God that we long for requires that we live out the expectations that come with this God-initiated relationship. One of those expectations is that we lovingly and faithfully care for our sisters and brothers, particularly those with greater needs than our own.

All of this we do because of who we are: a people redeemed, a people already transformed, a people reflecting the life that awaits us beyond this one. The Second Vatican Council made this point in a succinct and beautiful statement:

> Far from diminishing our concern to develop this earth, the expectation of a new earth should spur us on, for it is here that the body of a new human family grows, foreshadowing in some way the age which is to come. (Church in the Modern World 39)

That we expect life to continue beyond this one is the very reason for improving life here. We do so because we who live here are already the body of that new human family. We are already a reflection of that life to come. We just need to live as if we believe it. Part of that living is being good stewards of God's gifts within us, taking care of God's creation, and striving to build a more just community, nation, and world.

## ✍ Getting Practical

### Living Justly

The Scriptures tell us that justice has much to do with honoring the relationships into which we enter. Our movement to God requires both worship of God as well as loving actions toward our neighbor and compassion for persons in need. These biblical texts and the earliest Christian theologians remind us that if acts of worship are to be pleasing to God, they must lead to acts of charity and justice among our sisters and brothers who are marginalized. Modern Catholic social teaching challenges us to change anything in society and the world that prevents people from living a fully human life.

#### Living Faithfully Is Living Justly

The prophets of the Old Testament insisted that God expected the people of Israel to show particular care for the widows, orphans, and strangers. These were the poor and vulnerable people of that time and place. Israel's failure to show mercy and compassion to them was seen by the prophets as evidence that Israel was not living up to the covenant, that Israel's standing with God was deteriorating.

In the gospels we hear Jesus warn that responding to persons who are sick or hungry or abandoned in prison is a requirement of entry into God's kingdom. We would do well to ask ourselves how we might apply this teaching of Jesus and the prophets to our present setting. Who are the marginalized people of today? Who are the widows, orphans, and strangers of our time?

#### Fasting to End Hunger

Throughout Christian history, fasting enjoys a favored place among religious practices—as it does in Judaism and Islam. In all these religions fasting is more than an action we do out of a desire to come closer to God. Fasting also provides us with an opportunity to help other persons who have no food, persons whose lack of money and resources forces them to experience the pangs of hunger on a daily basis. How do we regard our fasting, especially during Lent? It might be helpful to meditate on the purpose of fasting and how well we practice this ancient call to Christians. Are we able to make the connection between refraining from full meals and offering financial aid to others so they may have a minimally adequate diet? Supporting organizations that address hunger might be a way for us to practice fasting in a way that helps many others. The very simple and practical Rice Bowl project of Catholic Relief Services during Lent is a wonderful model, not only for schoolchildren but for adults as well.

*Love Your Neighbor as You Change Society*

Catholic social teaching makes the case that to love our neighbor means to work for changes in society that allow this neighbor to live a better life. The parable of the Last Judgment provides a starting point for discussing these needs and the changes for us to consider—people are hungry and thirsty; they are sick and homeless. Are these also the issues of our day? Do these needs appear in the daily news?

A habit we might develop is to ask from time to time, what are the important issues of our day and how might we address them? More specifically, can we identify one improvement or change that we are able to help bring about? Let this be a change that will empower others to live more fully.

# Notes

1. Cyprian of Carthage, *On Works and Almsgiving* 5, in *Saint Cyprian: Treatises*, trans. Roy J. Deferrari, The Fathers of the Church: A New Translation 36 (Washington, DC: Catholic University of America Press, 1958), 231.

2. Ambrose of Milan, *On Naboth* 12.53, qtd. in Boniface Ramsay, *Ambrose*, The Early Church Fathers (New York: Routledge, 1997), 135.

3. John Chrysostom, *On Lazarus*, quoted in William J. Walsh and John P. Langan, "Patristic Social Consciousness—The Church and the Poor," *The Faith That Does Justice: Examining the Christian Sources for Social Change*, ed. John C. Haughey, Woodstock Studies 2 (New York: Paulist, 1977), 129.

4. Ambrose of Milan, *On the Duties of the Clergy* 1.28.132, in Nicene and Post-Nicene Fathers 2.10, ed. Philip Schaff and Henry Wace (Grand Rapids, MI: Wm B. Eerdmans, 1896).

5. *The Shepherd of Hermas* 3.5.3.7, in *The Apostolic Fathers*, trans. Francis X. Glimm, Joseph M.-F. Marique, and Gerald G. Walsh, The Fathers of the Church: A New Translation 1 (Washington, DC: Catholic University of America Press, 1947), 297.

6. Augustine, Sermon 100.7, quoted in "Patristic Social Consciousness," 118.

# PART II

# 4

# Personal Stewardship

Well done, good and faithful [servant]; you have been trustworthy in a few things, I will put you in charge of many things; enter into the joy of your master.

—Matthew 25:21

In its most fundamental sense stewardship means taking care of what belongs to God. This includes all of creation—humans and everything else God has placed in this world. As a matter of justice we practice stewardship in ways that bring hope and healing to a broken world, at home in our own communities and across the globe.

Essential to this practice of stewardship in a broad sense is that we take seriously our own development and movement toward God, that we practice personal stewardship. If we don't tend to our own well-being, we will have little to offer to other individuals or the various communities of which we are a part. Thus, to speak of sustained involvement in any type of stewardship presumes that we live in ways that make us physically able and spiritually motivated to concern ourselves with all of God's creation. It presumes that we are first serious about personal stewardship.

On a deeper level, however, personal stewardship is about our relationship with God. Being responsible stewards of our personal lives is a necessary part of our effort to be in a loving relationship with God who formed us to be what we are daily becoming. Personal stewardship is putting ourselves in a position to do the great things that God calls us to do in our family, community, church, and world. It is about developing and utilizing for God's purposes the abilities and gifts the Creator already has placed within us.

**Responding to God's Call**

The prophet Jeremiah provides insights into the nature of personal stewardship. He was an ordinary person called by God to accomplish a formidable task at a time when the nations surrounding Israel and Judah were undergoing war and social upheaval. His purpose would be that of announcing to Judah that devastating wars were coming—Yahweh's punishment for this people's unfaithfulness. Jeremiah objected to this calling, and resisted God's summons to take on this prophetic mission. He argued that he did not have the skills needed for this job, that he was not qualified to go before kings and princes and point out to them the many ways they had offended their God. He simply was not the one to tell the people (of Judah) that their covenantal relationship with Yahweh was broken and their doom was drawing near. Nor was this something he particularly wanted to do.

God's response was one of total reassurance: I am with you and I put my words in your mouth; I have created you for this task:

> Before I formed you in the womb I knew you,
> and before you were born I consecrated you;
> I appointed you a prophet to the nations. (Jer 1:5)

Before Jeremiah was born God assigned him this task—a very large one—to be a prophet to the nations, "to destroy and to overthrow, / to build and to plant" (1:10). Jeremiah's resistance ends. Not only must he take up the challenge God has placed before him, but he now does so with the confidence that God provides him all that he needs to succeed. Before his birth God consecrated him for this task and endowed Jeremiah with the human attributes to carry it out.

Each of us also has a calling to be a particular person, to do something unique with our lives. Each of us—like Jeremiah—has a vocation to live out and to do this with the awareness that God walks with us on this journey. We are given what is needed to live this calling and it is our responsibility to discover and nurture the gifts that have been planted in us since birth.

Sometimes those gifts may not be evident until later in life, sometimes only after we have suffered through a major loss and, in that process, discovered strengths and courage we didn't know we possessed. It is always inspiring to hear the story of a war veteran who lost one or more limbs but goes on to adjust his life and accomplish things for himself and his community. "I am with you. . . . Before I formed you in the womb I knew you."

For most of us, one of our first and continuing challenges is to live the Christian life. That is the context for learning how to guide our lives, for discovering what it means to practice personal stewardship in ways consistent with our vocation. This challenge is especially to live in this time and place as disciples of Jesus Christ. A most helpful way to live this discipleship is by being part of a faith community that proclaims the good news, that celebrates the presence of Christ in our midst, that supports and nurtures one another, and that reaches out in service and justice to a hurting world. Any one of these ministries offers the potential of drawing us more deeply into the Christian life and guiding us to fully use and develop the many gifts God has given us since the day of our birth.

It is not uncommon today to hear someone say, "I am spiritual but not religious. I prefer not to belong to any organized religion, church, or faith community." There may be no reason to question the sincerity of the person making this statement. Undoubtedly he or she is honestly seeking God in ways that tend to be individualized and private. What may be lacking in this effort, however, is the guidance and support that comes from other Christians traveling the same road. That companionship is essential when our journey takes some unexpected and undesired turns. It is also necessary throughout our lives to ensure that our faithfulness to God is always growing, as Jeremiah wished for the people of Judah.

Without the support of our faith community, our response to God is made more difficult. Without that support, we may not even grasp what this response entails—proclaiming, celebrating, nurturing, and serving. Learning all that the Christian life requires and offers is a lifelong education, one that must adjust as we move along, one that must take into account the ever-changing circumstances of our lives. God may have spoken directly to Jeremiah, and he may do so to us as well. But it is more likely that we will hear God's word through the voices of those with whom we gather to worship. From them we need to hear words of encouragement and correction if we are serious about understanding and answering God's invitation.

For this each of us was called. ("Before I formed you in the womb I knew you, / and before you were born I consecrated you.") In faith we accept that God gives us the gifts and talents needed to become more than we are at this moment. Our personal challenge is to make sure these talents do not go to waste. Our goal is to embrace a lifestyle that makes it possible for us to recognize and let flourish what we have received from our loving Creator. Ultimately the challenge is to respond to God's call and to do so with full use of the tools God has provided for this task. This is the practice of personal stewardship.

## Caring for Mind, Body, and Spirit

Personal stewardship is about taking our lives in the direction of mature and responsible moral persons. It does not require that we live like ascetics, as persons who feel compelled to live a life marked by daily penance, fasting, and limitless sacrifice. That may be the chosen and preferred lifestyle for some within the Christian community, but most of us are not called to that particular lifestyle.

The majority of Christians are called to live a full, rich, and satisfying life. This is not a life given to extremes or to personal advancement at the expense of others. It is not a life driven by the excesses of consumerism or a passion to prove our worth through purchasing power. Rather, this full, rich, and satisfying life derives from the experience of knowing that we are becoming the morally responsible persons that delight our Creator. A sure path to that experience is learning to recognize, value, and care for the gifts and talents with which God has blessed us.

This caring for mind, body, and spirit means living a life that is right for us. This will be a life that is satisfying and fulfilling on many levels, a life that has us maturing and flourishing as vibrant, joyful participants in God's wonderful creation. It will be a life that provides space and avenues for us to pursue particular passions and interests.

If we are attentive to what we have and who we are becoming, we will recognize and appreciate the various inclinations and interests that are part of our makeup. Following these interests and mastering the skills to do well in particular areas also are matters of personal stewardship. To do so is to honor and nurture what God already has planted within us.

Our interests, passions, and talents explain some of the differences among us, even among members of the same family. Some of us become construction workers, others bankers. Some work the land as farmers while others spend their time in courtrooms as lawyers and judges. Every profession, job, and career reminds us that each of us has our own path to follow, that the well-being of communities requires us to walk these paths, and that God has given us all we need for this journey.

This also means that no one should feel obligated to volunteer their time to work on one issue that others consider most important, whether that issue is visiting the homebound or affordable housing or abortion or gun control. Each of us has particular interests and passions around particular needs and challenges facing our church, society, and world. Each of us should use the skills and talents we possess to work on those issues. In so doing we not only remain faithful to our Creator in using the gifts we have received but we also ensure that all the needs and challenges of our time will be addressed. That is a common responsibility we share as a church and as a human community.

Another common responsibility is that of guiding ourselves to healthy lifestyles. This means that each of us responds to God's call by developing sound and healthy bodies, by letting our minds be sharp and challenged, and by making sure that our spiritual lives are rich and always growing. This care of mind, body, and spirit is not solely for our personal benefit even though we surely will enjoy the fruits of such efforts. As we consistently strive to keep ourselves healthy in every way, we know that others around us will benefit from what we are able to contribute to the well-being of the community.

Several years ago our parish sponsored small-group faith formation gatherings. I was delighted by how much I learned from other participants in the group to which my wife and I belonged—eight parishioners, mostly people who lived in our neighborhood. I was humbled and deeply moved by fellow parishioners' willingness to share the ups and downs of their faith journeys.

Personal stewardship directs us to contribute to the building of the Body of Christ, the church that Christ started before his death on the cross. That is part of the message in the text of 1 Corinthians:

> Now there are varieties of gifts, but the same Spirit; and there are varieties of services, but the same Lord; and there are varieties of activities, but it is the same God who activates all of them in everyone. To each is given the manifestation of the Spirit for the common good. (12:4-7)

The gifts that we possess, which we nurture and use for our personal growth and happiness, are destined also for the community's benefit. Whether we see "community" as the church or our town or the human family, we should recognize the social characteristics of our God-given talents and possessions.

In his 1987 encyclical, On Social Concern, Pope John Paul II spoke of the social obligations that come with the private ownership of property:

> Private property, in fact, is under a "social mortgage," which means that it has an intrinsically social function, based upon and justified by the principle of the universal destination of goods. (42)

John Paul II acknowledged the right to private ownership, but his principal interest was to underline the often overlooked truth that with ownership comes the obligation to use our possessions not only for our personal benefit but also to promote the good of the greater community.

A similar claim can be made regarding the talents and gifts God has given us. They are for our benefit, to guide us in responding to God's love, but that response includes paying attention to the building up of the body. A number of early Christian writers discussed this obligation in the context of some Christians being blinded by their passion for material wealth. The second-century Shepherd of Hermas pitied those rich persons who suffered from self-absorption and therefore were oblivious to the needs of the poor (3.10.4.2–3). In even stronger language St. Cyprian warned third-century Christians of the dangers of pursuing wealth at the expense of community mindedness:

> The deep and profound darkness of avarice has blinded your carnal heart. You are the captive and slave of your money; you are tied by the chains and bonds of avarice, and you whom Christ has already freed are bound anew.[1] (*On Works and Almsgiving* 13)

Cyprian and other theologians in the early church, like John Paul II in our time, used the topics of money and property to teach how Christians must be willing to place their resources at the service of others and of the larger community. Beyond financial and material resources, personal stewardship leads us to offer our talents and skills for the enrichment of the bodies in which we reside and flourish. This at times may require that we forego using our talents for personal advance when there is an opportunity to serve the interests of others.

Much of this discussion about using our gifts is summarized in an observation by Pope John XXIII in his 1963 encyclical, Peace on Earth:

> Individual citizens and intermediate groups are obliged to make their specific contributions to the common welfare. One of the chief consequences of this is that they must bring their own interests into harmony with the needs of the community. (53)

Living our lives in that manner will likely find us taking part in larger and more rewarding endeavors. The combination of foregoing self-interest and using our gifts to advance goals and projects bigger than ourselves can be incredibly rewarding. In many and varied ways we may find ourselves engaged in holy tasks—but only if we are practicing personal stewardship.

## Developing Our Gifts

Personal stewardship is about putting ourselves into a position where we are able to answer God's call in the midst of the demands that come with everyday living. In a general sense it demands that we live a healthy life and take good care of ourselves—mind, body, spirit. More specifically personal stewardship involves developing the particular talents and abilities that God has placed within us. The parable of the talents in Matthew 25:14-30 speaks to this point. In this story the master is about to go on a journey. Before leaving, he gives to his servants differing amounts of money (talents) to watch over and to make flourish. To one servant he gave five talents, to another two, and to another one. The parable tells us that the master gave "to each according to his ability," implying that the master expected the servants to do something worthwhile with the talents. It suggests as well that the master gave to the servants an amount that matched the capability of each. None of the servants could claim they lacked the skills, knowledge, or ability to make these talents grow, as the master expected.

Upon his return the master called each servant to account for his stewardship of the talents he had been given. The servants who received five and two talents had doubled the amounts originally given and the master praised them. But he who had received one talent buried it in the ground and now returned it alone to the master. The master was angry and he cursed this servant for not making better use of the talent he had been given. Then he took this one talent and gave it to the servant who now had ten talents, "for to all who have, more will be given."

This parable is a difficult text, one that has received various interpretations. What are we to make of verse 29, which has the master giving more to those who already have a lot and taking away "from those who have nothing"? And, how do we see honesty and integrity in this master who, according to the frightened servant receiving only one talent, is "a harsh man, reaping where you did not sow, and gathering where you did not scatter seed" (v. 24)? How do we explain Jesus using as the main character in this story a man who seems to be a little short on integrity? One lesson, however, seems clear from this story: to allow what we have been given to go unused and undeveloped is a very serious offense. Like the sorry servant with one talent, we at times may experience the fear of not performing up to all expectations: "I was afraid . . . you were a harsh man." Yet such fear cannot be an excuse for failure to work with the gifts we have received. That failure is a form of infidelity. It is a refusal to live up to the expectations of our relationship with God. It is a failure to respond to God's invitation, to use what God has placed within us to make that response possible. It is a failure of trust in God.

Nonuse of the gift leads to its diminishment and possibly even its loss—the master took away the one talent and gave it to the one with ten. Failure to develop and use our gifts may lead to extremely harsh consequences—the servant was expelled into darkness and suffering. Without reading this parable too literally, we might at least conclude that there likely will be some kind of reckoning on how well we did or did not employ the resources God made available to us. They are given for a purpose and they come with an expectation that we will use them. Being faithful to that expectation is not an option.

On the other hand, proper care and use of our gifts bring their own reward. "To all those who have, more will be given" (v. 29). This likely is not referring to money. Rather, the reward of fidelity, or in this parable the reward for the servants carrying out the expectations of their master, is the commission of greater responsibility. As we develop and use the talents we have been given, these talents are enriched and we are empowered even more to use them in faithful response to God's call and in the service of others.

Though not often noted, the parable of the Talents (Matt 25:14-30) immediately precedes the parable of the Last Judgment (Matt 25:31-34). Together the two parables offer a lesson about developing our gifts and using them on behalf of others. The parable of the Last Judgment calls us to serve others, especially "the least of my sisters and brothers." The parable of the Talents encourages us not to waste the gifts God has given us, but to develop them so that we have something to offer others.

## ✍ Getting Practical

### Responding to God's Presence

Developing and properly using the gifts God has given us requires work. It does not allow us to be content with just getting by in life. Rather, it beckons us to live as full a life as we possibly can, a life that is both balanced and yet open to new challenges and responsibilities. Several attitudes and activities are essential to living such a life.

*Prayer*

Prayer is about communicating with God, about being in the presence of God, and it is a requirement for personal stewardship. This deliberate attempt to communicate with God comes through both personal (private) prayer as well as liturgical (public) prayer. A life of prayer involves the habit of placing oneself in the presence of God and communicating with our Creator who desires and empowers us to become more than we are at this moment.

We know such prayer—such deliberate communication with God—is possible because through baptism we already are united with Christ. Whether praying with fellow believers through liturgical celebrations or in the privacy of our homes, prayer helps us develop a faithful and empowering relationship with God. It is in this relationship that we come to appreciate what God has given us and how we should use these gifts. This connectedness with God that develops through prayer eventually becomes the surest guarantee that we will not fear to use our talents in both simple and remarkable ways.

*Spirituality*

There are many ways to talk about spirituality. A helpful approach is to see it as recognizing that there is more to life than the ordinary happenings we think of as daily life. Spirituality involves an awareness that life is touched by the presence of God, even if we cannot explain how this is so. It carries a recognition that God is present in our lives in a transforming way. This is an active presence on the part of God, one that is constantly calling us to grow and to change.

Spirituality, then, is our response to God's transformative presence in our lives. It is a continuous and lifelong response and it involves our entire being. The more we attend to this response to God's presence in our lives, that is, the more we engage our spirituality, the more we become the people God calls us to be. Along this road we nurture and put to use every attribute that makes us who we are. That is living personal stewardship in a dynamic and life-giving way.

There are various ways for us to pursue a deeper spirituality, one that continually enriches every aspect of our lives. Regular conversations with a spiritual director proves to be helpful for many Christians. So do retreats of various types. Taking time out from the busyness of life to spend a weekend or a day in the quiet presence of God can be life-giving. It might be helpful to read a biography of a holy person who lived during this era, to ask how she or he maintained a relationship with God in life settings similar to our own.

## Recognizing Our Gifts

Saint Paul, as noted earlier, is particularly clear in writing to the earliest Christians about the nature of the gifts they have received. The origin and purpose of these gifts should not be in doubt; they are from the Spirit and for the common good. "To each is given the manifestation of the Spirit for the common good" (1 Cor 12:7). It is one and the same Lord who gives these gifts to all of us, activates them, and orients them to the good of the community. Our first task in identifying whatever gifts we find in ourselves is to acknowledge their source and their purpose. We have them because of God's generous love and because God trusts us to use them on behalf of the larger community.

In another text Paul stresses that our gifts vary according to the grace given us from God. Romans 12:4-11 notes that these gifts include prophecy, ministry, teaching, exhorting to ethical living, almsgiving, leadership, and acts of mercy. It is incumbent upon each of us to discover what gifts we possess, to let them develop and mature as we grow, and to place them at the service of the community. If each of us commits to this, then the many and varied gifts that the same Spirit has poured forth among all of us will be directed to the common good.

## Be an Active Part of the Body

One of the surest and most practical ways of using our gifts—of practicing personal stewardship—is by participating actively in the body. Here the body can mean our church as well as the different communities in which we find ourselves (area of residence, school, work). Our willingness to be active members of these bodies increases the likelihood that we will live out personal stewardship.

The more active we become, the more other members of the body will come to know us and the more they will help us to recognize our gifts. By listening to other members of our faith community—or our school, our family, our workplace— we learn where and how we can use our gifts. Oftentimes it will be our colleagues, in any of these bodies, who will see our gifts even before we have recognized them. It may also be these same persons who hold us accountable and admonish us when we do not make full and proper use of our gifts.

## Note

1. Cyprian of Carthage, *On Works and Almsgiving* 13, in *Saint Cyprian: Treatises*, trans. Roy J. Deferrari, The Fathers of the Church: A New Translation 36 (Washington, DC: Catholic University of America Press, 1958), 239.

# 5

# Stewardship of Our Gifts

Like good stewards of the manifold grace of God, serve one another with whatever gift each of you has received.

— 1 Peter 4:10

Stewardship leads us to recognize, develop, and use God's gifts within us. We use them to satisfy our own needs and those of our neighbor. The Gospel call to love our neighbor necessarily includes serving other people and there is no better way to do this than by using our gifts in responding to our neighbor's needs.

## Serve One Another

Stewardship of our gifts is about sharing our knowledge, talent, love, and expertise in service to others. Certainly we should tend to our own daily needs and strive to live a healthy and happy life. The point here is that we don't stop with ourselves but remain open to seeing others and especially to recognizing the mutual support we can be to one another. This attitude has us serving not only persons close to us and those with whom we feel comfortable. It likewise encourages us to enter into relationships with other persons whose needs we are in a position to address, and to refrain from making judgments that limit our response. On this last point Clement of Alexandria in the second century strongly warned his readers not to spend a lot of time making judgments about who was worthy of their assistance:

> You must not try to distinguish between the deserving
> and the undeserving. You may easily make a mistake,
> and, as the matter is in doubt, it is better to benefit
> the undeserving than, in avoiding this, to miss the
> good. We are told not to judge. We must open our
> generosity to all who are enrolled as disciples, paying
> no attention to appearance or condition or weakness
> or tattered clothes.[1]

Clement's concern here seems to be that the Christians of
his time (second century) be willing to assist other Christians
without trying to judge who is and is not deserving. As seen in
chapter 2, this practical expression of loving our neighbor—
using our gifts to serve others—was understood to include all
of our neighbors whether Christian or not.

Responding to our neighbor's needs through the use of
our gifts is the minimal requirement that flows from Jesus'
command that we love one another. This teaching is presented
simply but beautifully in the First Letter of Peter:

> Like good stewards of the manifold grace of God,
> serve one another with whatever gift each of you has
> received. (4:10)

Whatever talents and abilities we may possess, this passage
encourages us to use them in loving service of one another. To
live in this way distinguishes our present life in Christ from
any past inclinations to live solely for ourselves or to orga-
nize our daily activities under the single objective of bringing
happiness to ourselves. In itself that objective is not bad; it's
just not complete—at least not for one who professes to be a
follower of Jesus Christ.

To use our gifts in service of one another moves us in the
direction of living in the Spirit as the Gospel calls us to do.
This style of living colors all of our days. It may involve he-
roic moments of exceptional acts on behalf of others, like the
daily care and compassion Mother Teresa provided to the
dying poor in the streets of Calcutta. It may call us to follow

the example of Dorothy Day in advocating for the poor of America whose minimal well-being is so often ignored by the economic and political systems and by those who benefit from these systems. For many of us it may be as easy as doing the ordinary, simple things of daily living that bring joy and comfort to others in small, practical ways. It may take the form of intentional acts of love and kindness to persons who have a right to expect that from us—our children and parents, spouses and friends, those with whom we share classrooms and those with whom we share the workbench. All of this— the ordinary and extraordinary action, the great and small deeds—is the fruit of our willingness to serve others with the abilities and strengths God supplies. In doing this we practice stewardship of our gifts, and we glorify God.

Stewardship of our gifts on behalf of others says many things about how we live and how we relate our faith to daily living. On one level it represents a challenge to cultural notions of competitiveness and individualism, the popular dictum that tells us we should do everything we can to get ahead without much concern for our sisters and brothers also struggling on the same treadmill. This gospel orientation reminds us that winning is not everything and that true success is not something we achieve on our own, much less at the expense of others. This is not a message that finds a comfortable home in a society that places great value on "going it alone" and re-vering monetary success apart from full human development.

Using our abilities to serve others—stewardship of our gifts—demands constant attention and awareness of what is happening around us at any moment and in any location. It also calls for the development of good habits and practices to support this orientation. Such behavior is often modeled in families or within other important relationships, where we learn that we are loved and that we are capable of loving and serving others. It is in these loving contexts that we embrace the truth that we truly need to practice the art of loving actions toward others. This is the art of developing good habits, of living the virtue of charity. It is the simple act of letting God's gifts in us benefit others.

Beyond nurturing families there are other areas of our lives where we find structured and ready opportunities to use our talents for ourselves and for others. These include our local faith community, our parish. Through all of its ministries—worship, faith formation, fostering community, service, and justice—an effective parish offers constant instruction and motivation on service to others. That same parish likewise provides opportunities to practice this love of neighbor. The individual Christian's love of neighbor must not be limited to good intentions but must take life in actions. So also the Christian congregation and parish must not only preach and teach love of neighbor but must also provide opportunities for members to become active in serving others.

## Disciples of Jesus Christ

Stewardship of our gifts, especially in service to our neighbor, is a way of honoring God, who chose to endow us with particular capabilities. It also is a way of letting our lives reflect the reality that we are disciples of Jesus Christ. Saint John's gospel explains what this discipleship entails:

> For I have set you an example, that you also should
> do as I have done to you. (13:15)

The example to which John refers is Jesus' washing the feet of his disciples. This narrative appears to replace the account of the eucharistic Last Supper in this gospel. It suggests a strong connection between our participation in the Eucharist and our love of neighbor that leads to acts of service and justice.

Our participation in the eucharistic liturgy draws us into the community's praise and worship of God. Through this act of public worship we give thanks to God for what has happened to us through Jesus Christ. The death and resurrection of Christ have restored us to right relationship with God, with one another, and with all of God's creation. For this we give thanks, *eucharistia*, and we commit ourselves to go out from this celebration and work to change whatever contradicts this message of sisterhood and brotherhood among all of God's children. This particular ritual of thanksgiving reaches its conclusion in our actions after we leave the altar and become active in the world.

Saint Irenaeus of Lyons in his great second-century work, *Against Heresies*, noted this connection between Christians' celebration of the Eucharist and their willingness to serve their neighbor through acts of mercy, compassion, and justice. He wrote that this communal worship of God must be accompanied by an inner charity and justice toward one's neighbor or it will be of no avail. The eucharistic act must proclaim unity with God, with fellow human beings, and with the rest of creation (IV. 18, 3). The proclamation of unity must be active and visible, and it must effect positive change for individual persons or for the community, society, or larger world.

Closer to our day, the 1971 synod of bishops wrote that liturgy "is a thanksgiving to the Father in Christ, which through its communitarian form places before our eyes the bonds of brotherhood and again and again reminds us of the Church's mission." The paragraph concludes with the assertion that the Eucharist forms the community and places it at the service of all people (Justice in the World 58). The Eucharist continues through our presence in the world, a presence marked by a love and compassion that seeks expression.

The "service of all people" is the responsibility of the worshiping community and of each member of that community. We leave the eucharistic celebration with hearts ready to serve our neighbor using the talents and resources we are privileged to enjoy. These actions reflect what it means to be a disciple of Jesus Christ, to follow Christ's example, to "do as I have done to you." It is through such actions related to our celebration of the Eucharist that we live out Jesus' new commandment:

> I give you a new commandment, that you love one another. Just as I have loved you, you also should love one another. (John 13:34)

Jesus' death on the cross was made possible by his love for all of us, and in the cross he taught us how to love, not in comfortable and abstract ways that make no demands upon our lives. Rather, our love for one another, if it is to model the love of Christ, must show itself through practical here-and-now actions that allow our resources and capabilities to intersect with our neighbors' needs.

This is what baptism into Christ empowers us to do. It truly is possible for us to be followers of Christ, to live his teachings and to follow his example of loving others. This we can do through real-life decisions and actions from morning till nightfall. All of this we can do by using to the fullest extent the many talents we come to discover in ourselves, as we remember Jesus' words: "you also should love one another."

To seek to love as Christ loves is the characteristic mark of a Christian. Such love is grounded in ordinary living and engaged with the people around us because that is what Christians do. As the Letter to the Philippians states, "Let each of you look not to your own interests, but to the interests of others. Let the same mind be in you that was in Christ Jesus" (2:4-5). This is the kind of life that reflects good stewardship of our gifts. Through such a life we grow in spiritual and moral maturity and build up the Body of Christ, the church, our faith community. And, we give glory to God.

**One People**

Throughout our lives the accomplishments that we realize are almost always dependent upon other people. There is very little that we do alone, little that we achieve entirely by ourselves. We look to one another to bring about both small and large deeds to benefit ourselves, our families, and our communities. Stewardship of our gifts requires that all the resources of the community or household are directed toward the welfare of everyone.

As with life in communities, so our relationship with God is connected to and dependent on our relationship with one another. As noted in the earlier discussion about biblical justice, being in right relationship with God requires that we be in right relationship with our neighbor as exemplified in caring for the widows, orphans, and strangers of our time. It should not come as too much of an extension to say that our relationship with God is connected also to our neighbor's relationship with God. That is, my lifelong spiritual journey to live in God's friendship is associated with—perhaps even dependent upon—my neighbor's journey to this same God. The Second Vatican Council summarized this thinking in one simple and beautiful statement:

> God . . . "willed to make women and men holy and to save them, not as individuals without any bond between them, but rather to make them into a people who might acknowledge him and serve him in holiness." (Church in the Modern World 32)

God did not make us for life in isolation, apart from all other humans. There are some persons, certainly the exceptions, who thrive in relative isolation but even these share at least a minimal dependence on the services and structures that society provides. For the vast majority of us, however, interacting with one another and living with some degree of dependence upon our neighbors and the larger community is both the norm and a blessing. We don't have to do it all on our own.

We are a people—social creatures with needs that must be satisfied by other people just as we are there for the benefit of so many other individuals in our family, among our friends, and within our various communities. This is one of the most basic realities of our life in society. It is likewise the case that we need one another for our spiritual growth and moral development, and for our journey to God.

It is God who moves us toward holiness and justice, and it is God who saves us. This we all know and readily acknowledge. But it is equally important to recognize, in the second part of that Vatican II statement, that God makes us holy and saves us as a people. In the Hebrew Scriptures it was the people who entered into a covenant with God, not isolated individuals. Likewise, it was to the chosen people that the prophets declared the covenantal relationship between Yahweh and the Hebrew people to be broken. Today many Christians have a tendency to emphasize their personal relationship with Jesus Christ. The relationship that each of us has with Christ is important, and most of us give this far too little attention. At the same time we should acknowledge that throughout biblical and Christian history there has been a compelling awareness of the place of the community—the people—in each person's journey to God.

Jesus vividly demonstrated that loving one another means being present to one another, being willing to assist one another whatever the need may be. That must include our communal search for God. We go to God together and along the way we serve, guide, and help one another with whatever gifts each of us has received. This may well be the most important arena in which we practice stewardship of our gifts.

### Church and World

Living as one people, and serving one another within this human community, applies both to our life in the church and our life in the world. Our service to one another in the faith community involves both local and global stewardship. We are one people in our local parishes and congregations and we are connected and responsible for everyone within this local faith community. The parish itself depends upon each and every member's active engagement and support. The gifts of everyone in the congregation are needed for that parish to proclaim the Gospel effectively and to carry out all ministries. This never can be the sole responsibility of the pastor and the pastoral staff. Nor should it. Through baptism each of us is empowered to use our gifts for the sake of the Body. This is both a responsibility and a right, one we should eagerly embrace, not wait for members of the parish staff to beg us to make our talents available for the various parish ministries.

Yet, the stewardship of our gifts within the church must not be limited to the particular congregation wherein we are registered and worship. We are part of a global church and that church requires the support of every member in every corner of the world. How we provide that support depends upon the gifts, interests, and passions each of us has received.

Many among us provide that support through financial contributions and there are multiple channels within Christian denominations for doing this: Catholic Relief Services, Church World Service, the Catholic Campaign for Human Development. Others may use their talents in service of God's people by volunteering for a period of time to work in a mission program somewhere in the United States or in another country. However we do it, the value of our act is found in the fact that it benefits the church as a whole and that this act symbolizes the claim that stewardship of our gifts takes place within and on behalf of the entire church.

Our service to one another in the faith community leads us to service in the larger world. Jesus' command to love one another cannot be limited to fellow Christians as if only Christians are loved by God and thereby deserving of our love. All members of the human family are sons and daughters of the one loving God. All share in our human dignity and all are called to friendship with God. The love and service we show to our neighbor must be universal. That is the point made by Pope Paul VI in his 1975 apostolic exhortation, On Evangelization in the Modern World. We witness to the good news of the Gospel, we evangelize, through our acts of mercy and compassion directed toward people everywhere. Paul VI was clear that true evangelization must at some point proclaim through words the name, teachings, life, and mystery of Jesus of Nazareth. Still this Gospel also must be proclaimed by witness, a wordless witness through which "Christians stir up irresistible questions in the hearts of those who see how they live" (21).

> For the Christian community is never closed in upon itself. The intimate life of listening to the Word and the Apostles' teaching, charity lived in a fraternal way, the

sharing of bread—this intimate life only acquires its
full meaning when it evokes admiration and conversion, and when it becomes the preaching and proclamation of the Good News. (Evangelization in the
Modern World 15)

Stewardship of our gifts, using them to benefit anyone in God's
human family, becomes a witness to Christ in the world. It
becomes a way to proclaim the Gospel. The 1971 world synod
of bishops earlier identified working for justice anywhere in
the world as a manner of preaching the Gospel:

Action on behalf of justice and participation in the
transformation of the world fully appear to us as a
constitutive dimension of the preaching of the Gospel,
or, in other words, of the Church's mission for the
redemption of the human race and its liberation from
every oppressive situation. (Justice in the World 6)

Working to help create a world that more closely reflects the
love and mercy, the justice and peace of God is a way of proclaiming the Gospel to all corners of the earth. It is at the
same time one of the most important ways to love and serve
people everywhere.

Reaching out to anyone with needs is not only a requirement of our faith, it is not only a demonstration of the faith
we claim to profess, but it also is a way of announcing that
faith—of sharing the Gospel with the world. It is to this that
we direct whatever abilities and passions make up who we
are. It is in this way that we practice stewardship of our gifts.

## ✍ Getting Practical

### Letting the Community Guide Us in Using Our Gifts

Stewardship of our gifts—using them in ways that benefit
others—can be as simple as making ourselves available to others, responding as best we can to whatever needs we encounter.

It can also present a challenge requiring that we know what we are particularly good at and being able to recognize where our skills and talents are most needed. This also is a dimension of stewardship: using our talents in the best way possible. Most of us recognize this intuitively. How often someone remarks about a person that is so gifted and could do so much more with his or her life.

## Know and Use Our Gifts

Stewardship of our gifts begins with having an awareness of our strengths and interests. What are we good at and what are we passionate about? If we have a sense of that, then it will not be difficult to know where and how to be active in using these talents and abilities. We do this through the daily, ordinary responses to what comes across our path, and we let this become a habitual way of being present to others. By developing this habit—this virtue—of responding positively to people in ordinary circumstances, we prepare ourselves for the extraordinary actions that sometimes are needed. A step in this direction might be to reflect on when and where we are most likely to offer assistance to someone else, and which of our skills or gifts most often comes into play.

We also discover new ways to use our gifts as long as we are open to new directions and emerging needs. This is not always easy because most of us have a tendency to settle into comfortable actions, even when we are serving others. But there are many points in life that provide the opportunity to ask if we are using our abilities in the best way possible. These include changing our job or residence, joining a different congregation, graduating from high school, entering retirement, committing ourselves to one other person through marriage. These and many other "turning points" in life offer a new opportunity to ask again, What am I good at and what am I passionate about?

Ultimately this approach to stewardship of our gifts is about our growth and our spirituality. It is about how we respond to God's presence in our lives. Stewardship of our gifts is not about returning something to God (he doesn't need it), but about using what God has given us to ensure a reasonably decent life for ourselves and for serving others. In the process we may be acting our way into greater love of God, neighbor, and the rest of creation.

## Engage the Community

Not made to live in isolation, we are social and we need one another. Reaching out to others and volunteering in any program is valuable and at times it can be especially beneficial to do this with persons who share our faith commitments. This makes it possible to engage in theological reflection, to explore more deeply what we are doing and why. It allows us to sharpen our appreciation of the connection between faith and daily living and to do so in dialogue with persons who share our values. From time to time it might be helpful to review all of the ministries and programs that our parish offers. (These usually can be found on the parish website.) Which ones catch our attention and our interest? Which ones offer us new challenges?

The faith community can help us know our gifts and recognize where and how to use them since people around us often can see things about us that we may never have recognized. The parish community is made up of persons engaged in many different professions and life commitments. Many of them are in a position to inform us of new opportunities for us to consider as venues for making the best possible use of our talents.

Perhaps the greatest benefit we draw from our association with a faith community is that which includes both support and accountability. Members of our congregation can challenge us to use our gifts, but only if we are at least somewhat involved in the life of our parish. If the parish is healthy, members will encourage one another to be active and to respond to needs on a regular basis. They will help one another recognize the talents that are present within the community and they will hold one another accountable. If we allow this to happen on a regular basis, then it likely also will be done during extraordinary moments when the risks are greater but the rewards and potential for growth are as well. That can provide an especially opportune moment for being good stewards of our gifts.

# Note

1. Clement of Alexandria, *Quis Dives Salvetur* 33, in R. B. Tollinton, *Clement of Alexandria: A Study in Christian Liberalism*, vol. 1 (London: Williams and Norgate, 1914), 318.

# 6

# Local Stewardship

[F]or those who do not love a brother or sister whom they
have seen, cannot love God whom they have not seen.

— 1 John 4:20

Stewardship means taking care of what belongs to God—all
of creation including ourselves and our neighbor. Caring for
our neighbor, using our gifts to empower others, is a requirement of justice. It also is an expectation of our loving God.
The First Letter of John explains why this is so:

> We love because he first loved us. Those who say, "I
> love God," and hate their brothers or sisters, are liars;
> for those who do not love a brother or sister whom
> they have seen, cannot love God whom they have not
> seen. The commandment we have from him is this:
> those who love God must love their brothers and sis-
> ters also. (4:19-21)

John's message is simple and direct, building as it does on
Jesus' two great commandments: "You shall love the Lord
your God with all your heart, and with all your soul, and with
all your mind" and "You shall love your neighbor as yourself"
(Matt 22:36-40). In John's statement we find a blunt reminder
of what the gospels repeatedly assert, that is, love of God and
love of neighbor cannot be separated. Anyone who claims to
do so is a liar. It is simply impossible to love God if we do not
love the neighbor in front of us.

In connecting love of God and love of neighbor John provides the rationale for local stewardship. In a universal sense we love our neighbor because God has loved us first, and demonstrated that love through the death of his beloved son. In more immediate terms we also must love in practical ways the brothers and sisters whom we see before us in our churches or communities or wherever our lives take us. We must love the neighbor we see in our day-to-day encounters—we must practice local stewardship.

## Responding to What Is in Front of Us

Our love of God leads us to acknowledge and honor the dignity of every person—to affirm that every person we meet is a child of God for whom Christ has won redemption and offered the hope of eternal happiness with God. We expect that every person at some level desires to respond to this invitation to new life and to salvation from all that prevents us from enjoying the company of God. Within that outlook it seems reasonable to assume that all people strive to live a good life, a life marked by high moral conduct and by an ever deepening spiritual life. Those are among the minimum of expectations embedded in our relationship with God.

From a slightly more negative vantage point we also acknowledge, as the Second Vatican Council reminded us, that fulfilling these expectations and fully responding to God's love require living conditions that support our growth and development as persons blessed from birth with a sacred dignity. Sadly, those social, cultural, economic, and political conditions for supporting a dignified life are not always present in every community. This certainly is the case in many countries around the world, and it is the case here in the United States. For that reason alone every one of us has an obligation to help create those conditions in the neighborhoods and communities where we live and work. We have an obligation to practice local stewardship.

Responding to what is in front of us is a sound way to practice stewardship in any form, because it is local, daily, and familiar. It is worth noting that, according to the Gospel of Luke, Jesus began his public ministry in his hometown, among people who knew him. There, in the synagogue in Nazareth, he read from the prophet Isaiah the words that foretold his work:

> The Spirit of the Lord is upon me,
>     because he has anointed me
>         to bring good news to the poor.
> He has sent me to proclaim release to the captives
>     and recovery of sight to the blind,
>         to let the oppressed go free,
> to proclaim the year of the Lord's favor. (Luke 4:18-19)

His listeners were amazed at what he had to tell them following this reading, especially since he was one of their own. "Is not this Joseph's son?" Of course, after Jesus developed the point that no prophet is accepted in the prophet's hometown, the people promptly led him to the hill "so that they might hurl him off the cliff" (v. 29).

The risks and rewards of local stewardship are easily apparent. As the Gospel of Luke makes clear, trying to make a difference among people we know can invite resistance simply because we are known—our families, our work, our own shortcomings. On the positive side, focusing on local needs likely will allow us to work on problems or challenges with which we are quite familiar. The proximity of these projects or human needs provides us with the opportunity to respond or engage them on a more regular basis. These may be local needs that we simply didn't notice in the past or possibly chose to ignore. If we are serious about using our abilities to improve lives beyond our own, if we are serious about caring for what belongs to God, then we might begin by responding to what is in front of us.

That response to our neighbor's need must be practical. We do not love our neighbor in the abstract. Our love must be as concrete and practical as are his or her needs and as are Jesus' actions in the gospels. The signs of the nearness of the reign of God that Jesus manifested were actions related to what people were lacking at that moment: a healthy body for the centurion's son in Capernaum, bread and fish for the five thousand, restored sight to the two men outside Jericho. As disciples of Jesus, we need to ask, What are the needs in my neighborhood or region that I might be in a position to help alleviate? This is more than a Christian obligation. It is allowing ourselves to act as Jesus did, with love and empathy to all we meet. As the Gospel of Matthew puts it, Jesus cured the two blind men because he was "moved with compassion" (20:34).

Local stewardship is carrying out these acts of mercy and compassion to the neighbor we encounter every day here at home. When performed out of love, they are a witness to the nearness of the reign of God, and to our acceptance of Jesus' call to repent and believe in the good news. They become a testimonial to our conviction that nothing in life is more important than our love of God and the new life this love offers— a love manifested in acts of compassion toward our neighbor. "[F]or those who do not love a brother or sister whom they have seen, cannot love God whom they have not seen."

A test of our love and faith is found in these daily acts of kindness and compassion that we extend to brothers and sisters around us. The Letter of James describes it well:

> What good is it, my brothers and sisters, if you say you have faith but do not have works? Can faith save you? If a brother or sister is naked and lacks daily food, and one of you says to them, "Go in peace; keep warm and eat your fill," and yet you do not supply their bodily needs, what is the good of that? So faith by itself, if it has no works, is dead. (2:14-17)

James seems to presume we are in a position to help, or at least he is referring to those situations where that is the case. It is difficult to imagine that we are never in such a position of being able to extend loving-kindness and practical assistance to people we meet throughout the day. Our faith, then, requires a response at such moments in line with our capabilities. The issue here is not about the relative importance of faith and works, much less about whether we in some way earn salvation through our good deeds. Rather, the point is that if we have faith in Jesus Christ, that faith will be evident in the acts of love that we show toward others. In the language of the Hebrew Scriptures, if our standing with God is good, it will prove itself in our care for the widows, orphans, and strangers.

Practicing local stewardship—using our talents and resources to help people around us—flows from our love of God, from our absolute trust and faith in Jesus Christ. It also indicates that we understand what it means to be a Christian, that we are willing to do as Christ did by loving our sisters and brothers in ways that respond to their concrete needs.

The gospels make clear that our neighbor is anyone and everyone. Jesus' command to love our neighbor allows no limits or boundaries that can exclude any individual or group. The concept of neighbor is now universalized. In the context of local stewardship we might consider the neighbor to be anyone whose need we see and are in a position to aid. This may feel like a stretch and certainly can be an awkward Christian responsibility to carry out on a regular basis. Yet Pope Benedict XVI stressed this point in his first encyclical:

> Anyone who needs me, and whom I can help, is my neighbor. The concept of neighbor is now universalized, yet remains concrete. (God Is Love 15)

The Holy Father challenges us to think a little differently about our neighbor and about our relationship to him or her. To recognize another person's need requires some minimal connection to that person. It suggests a relationship that is more dynamic than static, one in which we are at least able to recognize when someone is in difficulty or is lacking something required for a decent life. As noted earlier, we all need one another, especially the persons living or working or studying or worshiping alongside of us. These are our neighbors whom we may be in a position to assist, just as they can support us in various ways. That said, we are not likely to reach out and respond to another's need unless we are "moved by compassion." That powerful motivating compassion may take hold of us more readily if we already have a caring relationship with the other.

The neighbor remains a real person whether living next door or on the other side of the planet. In either case, the neighbor is not an abstraction, especially the one with whom we have regular contact. That neighbor can help us learn how to love as Jesus commanded, without judging and without being overly concerned about results.

A dear friend of mine, Fr. Jack Davis, has worked in an impoverished parish in Chimbote, Peru, for more than thirty-eight years. Every morning people line up at the parish gates to ask him for money to buy food or medicine or school supplies. Every morning Fr. Jack gives what money he has to those asking. Every morning he responds as best he can to overwhelming needs, knowing that some among these supplicants will return tomorrow. Americans visiting Fr. Jack's parish, Our Lady of Perpetual Help, are sometimes unsettled by his quick response to the requests of these desperately poor people. Some visitors feel there should be more accountability demanded, more verifying of need before providing money, more checking to see that the money given was used properly. They may have an argument, especially from an American business perspective, but Fr. Jack seems to know what the Gospel calls for. To recall the advice of Clement of Alexandria, "You must not try to distinguish between the deserving and the undeserving. You may easily make a mistake, and, as the matter is in doubt, it is better to benefit the undeserving than, in avoiding this, to miss the good" (*Quis Dives Salvetur* 33).

Obviously there is a place for accountability in the use of our gifts and in the sharing of our abundance with others. Good stewardship by definition requires that we not waste or use foolishly the resources that God has allowed us to watch over. That position, however, can never become a justification for any Christian's failure to respond. Such inaction as well as being overly cautious when faced with another person's needs simply are not compatible with the expectations that accompany discipleship of Jesus Christ. To paraphrase St. Clement, when the matter is in doubt, it is better to give and be wrong than to hold back and deny someone what he or she has a right to ask from us.

Love and service of our neighbor is central to our identity as Christians, and it should happen especially among those neighbors who are near and around us. Failure to use our talents and resources to help the brother and sister whom we can see contradicts what it is to be a Christian. We must be clear on this, that even faithful churchgoing cannot compensate for a failure to love our neighbor. To love our neighbor in practical ways is no less important than our acts of worship, as the Old Testament prophets warned when they condemned ritual acts that did not lead to just living. Again, Pope Benedict spoke to this point with unmistakable clarity: "The Church cannot neglect the service of charity any more than she can neglect the Sacraments and the Word" (God Is Love 22).

The church is both the people of God and the institutional church with its ordained leaders and parish staffs. Included in this certainly is the local parish or congregation. This church and these church members must celebrate the sacraments, proclaim the Gospel, and reach out in charity and justice to neighbors both near and far. All of these constitute the mission of the local parish and are usually present in mission statements posted on parish websites. None of these ministries can be neglected if the church—the parish—is to realize its mission. And, all of these ministries are the responsibility of every parishioner, including that of charity and justice to nearby neighbors—the practice of local stewardship.

### Shaping Our Communities

There are many ways to practice local stewardship, many ways to use our resources to help persons in our neighborhood, community, or region. This may involve direct responses to peoples' needs here and now, and it may include efforts to improve our community and its institutions so that they better serve everyone. Among these are the time-honored corporal works of mercy where we seek to bring comfort to persons who are sick or lonely, or contribute money, food, clothing, or anything else that helps people meet their basic needs now. Another is volunteering our time in programs where we have a particular interest and where we may be able to offer special assistance because of our own talents. This is an especially rich form of local stewardship because it allows us to be personally engaged in efforts to help someone enjoy a better life.

To be directly involved in a project or organization aimed at improving our community places us in a position where we ourselves are likely to change. The same is true when we directly assist a person or group with particular needs that match our gifts and passions. In all these settings the assistance and benefits flow in both directions, to the one receiving the help and to the one offering it. The latter may gain a deeper or even new appreciation for why the persons being helped are in such need. When we offer our hand in assistance and friendship to another, we are at the same time inviting that person into our world. That has the potential to change us in countless ways—our attitudes about marginalized persons, our understanding of how our society's social, economic, and political systems don't function to benefit everyone, our awareness of how we may be contributing to the marginalization of people we now seek to help.

Local stewardship that has us directly engaged in efforts to improve the lives of others may lead us to profound spiritual transformation as well. Spirituality, as stated earlier, has something to do with our response to God's transformative presence in our lives, God's constant calling us to grow and to change. God may not call out to us in quite the same way he spoke to Jeremiah or Job. But God does speak to us, and quite often through the people he places in our lives.

Early Christian writers were sensitive to this reality, especially the likelihood that God speaks through neighbors whose unmet needs invite us into their lives and call us to change in the process. Clement of Alexandria observed in the second century that wealthy Christians should surround themselves with a band of paupers. He noted that the poor can provide a positive service to the rich—giver and receiver, rich and poor forming one community of support and sharing. And then, his dramatic imagery of how the poor serve those better off:

> The aged, the orphans, the widows, the men who wear the uniform of love, you will select to be your spiritual bodyguard, unarmed, unstained with blood, your sure defense against shipwreck or disease or robber's attack or demon's might.[1]

These are the people, Clement maintained, who can keep us grounded. They are the people of any age who struggle on a daily basis to have what is required for a minimally decent life—those who are elderly and without family living nearby, the ones who never seem to have enough food to set before their children or medicine to cure recurring ailments, a few others whom the community tends to avoid because they act out their mental demons, and the many who go from day to day grateful that they have jobs and incomes adequate to satisfy modest lifestyles. These are the people in any of our communities who can remind us of what is important in life and the values that should inform our own choices and behaviors. These are our neighbors whose lives might guide us to ongoing conversion toward the humility and simplicity of life presented to us in the gospels.

In 1971 I joined the national staff of a program that was coming into being in the Catholic Church called the Campaign for Human Development. Its purpose would be to provide millions of dollars in self-help and social change projects in poverty communities throughout the United States; and to design attitudinal change, social justice education projects, and materials for use in Catholic parishes. During my ten years with this wonderful program one of the greatest lessons I learned had to do with how best to change attitudes, stereotypes, and outright prejudices about poor and minority people. We designed and distributed a lot of material for use in parish religious education as well as adult faith formation programs. Yet none of this was as effective in changing attitudes among Catholic parishioners as creating opportunities for parishioners to have direct contact and involvement with persons struggling to live their lives free of poverty. Surrounding ourselves with Clement's aged, orphans, widows, and persons "who wear the uniform of love" can be an insurance for Christians seeking to stay on the right course.

That also can happen when we commit to local stewardship in ways that have us involved in projects or directly helping individuals or groups. The potential for the recipients of our kind gestures having a transformative impact on us is high. The voice of our ever present God can be heard among those we may label as poor, but who are indeed rich with the love of the one God who has demonstrated a particular love for widows, orphans, and strangers.

Local stewardship can lead to some remarkable changes within ourselves. It also directs us to promote the common good in those communities where we live, to help create those conditions in society that make it possible for everyone to do reasonably well. This kind of stewardship benefits all of us because it has us taking responsibility for our communities—our neighborhood, our city, our state.

It also has us working for changes that will benefit everyone, especially changes that make it more likely for people to have their basic needs met. This might take the form of changes in economic structures and practices that make it easier for people to find jobs, or to earn a living wage at the jobs they have. It could be changes in social policies that will ensure everyone has access to needed medical services. It also might be reform of the tax system to make tax rates progressive while providing public agencies the revenue they need to carry out their responsibilities. Some of these activities may involve advocating for public policy changes at the national level, but all of these impact our local communities and our next-door neighbor.

It is not always easy to see the connection between direct service (charitable acts) and systemic change (social justice), especially in the context of local stewardship. It may be helpful to recall the lesson of the parable of the Last Judgment:

> Then the King will say to those at his right hand, "Come, you that are blessed by my Father, inherit the kingdom prepared for you from the foundation of the world; for I was hungry and you gave me food, I was thirsty and you gave me something to drink, I was a stranger and you welcomed me, I was naked and you gave me clothing, I was sick and you took care of me, I was in prison and you visited me." (Matt 25:34-36)

Christian discipleship requires us to help any person who needs us and whom we are in a position to help. This may take the form of direct service that provides for someone's need here and now. Or, it may see us working for changes that will address the neighbor's long-term welfare.

In either case we should note that the parable of the Last Judgment makes such behavior a criterion for entry into the kingdom of God. The story offers examples that we today would tend to consider direct services: providing food, water, and clothing; ministering to persons who are ill; visiting others who are in prison. Yet we need to be careful about omitting social change actions from our response to the neighbor in need. John's gospel helps us see why this is so:

> I give you a new commandment, that you love one another. Just as I have loved you, you also should love one another. By this everyone will know that you are my disciples, if you have love for one another. (13:34-35)

To be followers of Jesus Christ, to be Christians, means above all that we love one another because God has loved us. It is tempting to see this love of neighbor as being satisfied by acts of service, especially since the example of loving one another that John provides in this chapter is Jesus washing his disciples' feet. But we must see that love of neighbor is not always satisfied by meeting his or her need at this moment, particularly so when we have the abilities and resources to do more.

True love of neighbor means we seek that person's long-term benefit and bring about whatever changes are needed to ensure that person's good on into the future. On this point, once again, Pope Benedict XVI is clear:

> The individual who is animated by true charity labors skillfully to discover the causes of misery, to find the means to combat it, to overcome it resolutely. (Charity in Truth 30)

True charity, true love of neighbor, moves us to help our neighbor with his or her immediate needs—an hour or two of visiting, referral to a homeless shelter, a financial contribution for food or a winter coat or school supplies for his or her children. And it goes beyond that. As Pope Benedict stated, love of neighbor requires us to ask why this person needs help with these items, and what we can do to address the causes of these problems. It may find us advocating for systemic changes that will make it more likely that these present needs today will be satisfied on into the future.

Using our gifts to serve others is a way toward empowering some persons who presently live on the margins of society. This is an empowerment that allows them to take charge of their own lives, to be less dependent upon others for daily needs. Ultimately it can lead to persons experiencing anew the development of their own gifts. When that happens, such persons are in a strong position to make their own contributions to the community and to the larger society. Local stewardship carries the wonderful potential of discovering countless unused gifts within our communities. When that is realized, everyone benefits.

# ✍ Getting Practical

## Serving Those around Us

Loving our neighbor in practical, effective ways can be challenging. Acknowledging that there are unmet needs in our neighborhood is difficult. Most of us like to think we live in communities where everyone is doing well. Likewise, it can be equally challenging to assist nearby residents without judging. That is especially why the practice of local stewardship needs to be a daily, habitual action on our part. There are various ways for us to engage this challenge with relative comfort.

### *Education and Advocacy*

Much of the tension existing between different population groups in any neighborhood or city is rooted in fear, misunderstanding, and false perceptions. Too often those conditions are allowed to continue fueling tensions. We are not naturally inclined to get involved in a matter that is controversial or messy or that may require us to take sides. Yet that is precisely what our faith calls us to do—to work for peace within our community, to promote respect and dignity for everyone.

One of the ways for us to move in that direction is to become as informed as possible about any group that seems to be living on the margins of our community, whether these groups differ from the majority because of income, race, religion, or any other characteristic by which the dominant population defines them. Our willingness to understand other people and honor their traditions can position us well to educate others by debunking stereotypes and easing tensions within the community. Most important, our efforts might help persons in marginalized groups to feel like welcomed and valued members of the community.

### *Creating Bridges between Communities*

Local stewardship means using our gifts to serve our nearby neighbors directly while also making connections with organizations, legislators, and other persons in positions to enact needed changes in the community. We cannot do this by ourselves as individual Christians or even as single parishes. The best use of our gifts in working for needed change may be in building bridges between the many persons, programs, and organizations that have an interest in community improvements. Working with others can also help avoid a feeling of being overwhelmed by the enormity of the challenges.

There are various ways to build such bridges. Developing a working relationship between our congregation and one in a less affluent part of our community can lead to rewarding consequences. At the least it is a way to learn the struggles of others and from them to learn what needs to be done. It may also reveal information we would rather not hear, like how we may be contributing to their problems in some way, or how the people in the less affluent parish may perceive us and how we function as a church.

Our parish can support the efforts of our diocesan or judicatorial social justice program. We may connect with the State Catholic Conference or local interfaith communities found through the National Council of Churches. Another option is to become part of an interfaith effort to impact state legislation around social justice issues (such as the Joint Religious Legislative Coalition in Minnesota, in which people of diverse faiths mobilize religious communities to influence public policy in Minnesota).

## Personal Engagement—Personal Conversion

Spirituality relates to how seriously we are willing to respond to God's transforming presence in our lives, to see how eagerly we take up Jesus' summons to repent and believe the good news. We might not easily see our spiritual growth as connected to our efforts at helping our neighbor, but that is a connection we would do well to make. If using our skills and resources engages us directly in some way with a person or group we wish to help, the likelihood of us being changed is quite strong. Our own conversion may come through reading, meditation, and prayer. It also comes through the stories, suffering, and struggles of other people in whom we see the face of God.

It might be the start of a transforming journey for us to consider spending time with a person who is suffering for any reason, someone who is not well received in our community, a person or family struggling to provide daily food or a place to sleep each night. What might we learn through this experience about that person's journey? How are we connected to his or her struggle? What can we do to help change their situation? What does this experience tell us about how we need to change? There are many opportunities for any of us to become engaged in this way. A good place to start is with our parish or diocesan social ministry staff, asking what local projects they could recommend for us to support and spend some of our time.

## Note

1. Clement of Alexandria, *Quis Dives Salvetur* 34, in R. B. Tollinton, *Clement of Alexandria: A Study in Christian Liberalism*, vol. 1 (London: Williams and Norgate, 1914), 318.

# 7

# Global Stewardship

But a Samaritan while traveling came near him; and
when he saw him, he was moved with pity.

—Luke 10:33

Local stewardship bids us to use our resources on behalf
of the neighbor who is in front of us—the one in our neighborhood, state, and country. This kind of stewardship holds
promise for our formation as responsible Christians because
of the direct contact it provides us with those we help. It also
is one expression of the larger biblical call to stewardship, a
call that directs us to let our gifts serve our neighbor anywhere
in the world, a call to practice global stewardship.

The parable of the Good Samaritan in Luke's gospel (10:29-
37) offers a basis for reflecting on global stewardship. A trav-
eler is robbed, beaten, and left to die in a ditch. He is ignored
by a passing priest and a Levite who share his nationality,
race, and religion. But then comes a Samaritan, one whom
Jews look upon with contempt and with whom they are to
have no contact. This Samaritan stops and assists the victim,
a Jew. The Samaritan interrupts his journey and goes to the
beaten man in the ditch. He pours oil on the man's wounds
and bandages them. Then he puts the man on his donkey and
takes him to an inn, where the man is cared for at the expense
of the traveling Samaritan.

An obvious message in this story is that Jesus expects us
to show love and compassion across all lines: race/ethnicity,

gender, age, or geography. Our acts of mercy are for everyone and must never be limited to persons within our family or friendship circles, much less to people who think, look, or behave like us.

This parable also suggests three critical points for understanding why we should practice global stewardship: we are to be in solidarity with all people; there is a universal purpose inherent in all created goods; and, we are to help those most in need.

## Solidarity

The virtue of solidarity leads us to live as one human family. All of us—whoever we are and wherever we live—share the same dignity from being created in the image of God. We are all redeemed through the life, death, and resurrection of Jesus Christ, and we all are called to communion with God. Though it may express itself in various ways, each of us seeks the same happiness in this life and in the one to come. All the while we struggle to live a dignified life regardless of location, race, sex, or religion.

It is also the case that each of us bears responsibility for other members of this human family. This is a responsibility that stretches beyond our immediate families and other close relationships. It is, in fact, one that goes beyond geographical boundaries. If we fully grasp the implications of this belief that we are connected to every other human being, then we will commit ourselves to the good of everyone, of every individual person, of every nation. It does not require us to abandon the special concern and responsibilities we have for our family members and others close to us, nor even for our neighborhoods and our nation. Meeting those obligations, however, must not happen at the expense of other members of the human community or of other nations. The welfare of other countries is something we embrace and seek to promote, not at the expense of our nation but as part of our solidarity with all peoples.

That commitment to the well-being of people everywhere is a requirement of our faith. The parable of the Last Judgment in Matthew 25 suggests that our entry into eternal happiness is dependent upon such merciful behavior. This was a theme that recurred in the works of early Christian writers, like the third-century bishop of Carthage, St. Cyprian. Addressing the Christians' obligation to show mercy to their neighbors, especially the poor among them, Cyprian directed his reader's attention to Isaiah 58: "Is not this the fast that I choose: / to loose the bonds of injustice, . . . to let the oppressed go free, . . . to share your bread with the hungry, / and bring the homeless poor into your house" (vv. 6-7)? These acts of mercy represent the ethical expectations that define what it means to be a disciple of Jesus Christ. Among those expectations is our willingness to be in solidarity with all people and to show compassion and mercy. Cyprian summarizes his reflection on Matthew 25 with the stark observation that God will show mercy only to the merciful (*On Works and Almsgiving* 5).

All of this may seem idealistic and impractical but it flows directly from Jesus' command to love our neighbor:

> "Teacher, which commandment in the law is the greatest?" He said to him, "'You shall love the Lord your God with all your heart, and with all your soul, and with all your mind.' This is the greatest and first commandment. And a second is like it: 'You shall love your neighbor as yourself.' On these two commandments hang all the law and the prophets." (Matt 22:36-40)

It is tempting to claim that by "neighbor" Jesus meant only those actually living in our neighborhood or proximate community. But his parable of the Good Samaritan does not seem to allow for such a constricted way of defining our neighbor. Jesus' command to love our neighbor is universal; it includes everyone everywhere. The call to love our neighbors is not only universal but practical as well. Our loving actions must be real.

Jesus modeled this love of neighbor on many occasions. He cleansed the lepers of a very real disease. He likewise healed the servant of a Roman centurion. He forgave a prostitute and he dined with a tax collector. Each of these acts of love, mercy, and compassion were responses to real-life happenings on the part of specific individuals he encountered in his ministry. And, we should note, these acts of mercy, these practical acts of love, were often directed toward persons normally looked upon as "outsiders." Jesus' acts of compassion offer a glimpse of how to practice global stewardship even in our daily encounters, showing hospitality and generosity toward every person we meet, not just those who look, act, or believe like we do.

Catholic social teachings build on the Good Samaritan parable and the examples of Jesus when they call us to use our gifts on behalf of people everywhere. These teachings lend a positive tone to the meaning of solidarity in the context of practicing global stewardship. Pope John Paul II, perhaps more than any pontiff, explicates the various ways we should understand solidarity as a way to live the Christian expectation to love our neighbor. His 1987 encyclical, On Social Concern, states that the demands for justice can only be satisfied on a global level. He questions how we can justify "huge sums of money" being spent "for the enrichment of individuals or groups, or assigned to the increase of stockpiles of weapons." This is a tragedy because we know that "war and military preparations are the major enemy of the integral development of peoples" (10).

From the perspective of global stewardship John Paul II asserts that our priorities are upset. A path to correcting this is one that leads us to appreciate more deeply our connectedness to the entire human family, what he refers to as the virtue of solidarity. This is "a *firm and persevering determination* to commit oneself to the *common good*; that is to say to the good of all and of each individual, because we are *all* really responsible *for all*" (38). His reflection concludes by noting that peace throughout the world ultimately is the fruit of justice and solidarity, not war or a reliance on military weapons.

Solidarity is the virtue that guides our practice of global stewardship and it helps us to rethink how we as individuals and as a nation view the world and our place in it. This virtue, this good habit, empowers us to see other people and other nations—especially people who live in poverty—not as problems but as fellow builders of a new and more human future for all of us. Solidarity represents a fresh new way of thinking about relations among nations and how the global community can best secure justice, development, and peace. At its core it is rooted in the conviction that we are all responsible for one another, and that we must practice global stewardship.

## Universal Purpose of Created Goods

In our earlier reflection on justice we noted the early Christian principle that all created goods serve a universal purpose. This teaching emerged out of patristic attempts to address the challenge of reconciling the presence of both poverty and wealth within early Christian communities. These third- and fourth-century Christian theologians taught that everything God has provided through creation is intended to satisfy the needs of all people. From this thinking it follows that Christians especially should be willing to share with anyone in need. In one of his homilies St. John Chrysostom laid out one of the practical implications of this teaching:

> [The rich] hold the goods of the poor even if they have inherited them from their fathers or no matter how they have gathered their wealth.[1]

Whatever we possess, whatever resources we enjoy, we should regard these earthly possessions as goods God meant both for our own needs and enjoyment and for meeting the needs of our neighbors, near and far, who may not be doing as well.

This idea receives further expression in modern Catholic social teachings when they speak of the right of desperately poor persons to take from the abundance of others, and when they consider the right to private ownership. A statement from Pope Paul VI in 1967 exemplifies this development:

> Private property does not constitute for anyone an
> absolute and unconditional right. No one is justified
> in keeping for his exclusive use what he does not need
> when others lack necessities. (On the Development of
> Peoples 23)

Clearly Paul VI lays out an exceptionally strong warning on
both the possession and the use of material goods beyond our
needs. Other persons, groups, or nations struggling to feed
their people and to provide life's basic necessities have some
claim upon those resources of ours that are not needed to satisfy what we require for a modest lifestyle. This is a difficult
teaching to hear and one of the most challenging to practice in
our lives. That said, it is important for every Christian to pursue
a lifestyle marked by this awareness that God's creation and all
he has provided within it are here to meet the needs of everyone. To live in this manner is to practice global stewardship.

Paul VI had a focus on global relationships. He was the
first pope in modern times to travel extensively, especially to
developing countries, and that direct exposure to global poverty is reflected in this encyclical. On many points his writings
bring us face-to-face—often in blunt, disturbing ways—with
the Christian's responsibility for global stewardship.

This universal purpose of the goods of creation as a foundation for global stewardship connects us with Jesus' command
to love our neighbor—practically and universally. Such a love
is tied to our love of God. That is, we cannot love God without
loving our neighbor. The First Letter of John makes that point
with disturbing clarity:

> How does God's love abide in anyone who has the
> world's goods and sees a brother or sister in need and
> yet refuses help? (3:17)

Today it is difficult to claim that we are ignorant of the
tremendous suffering and needs people face throughout our
world. We know, for example, that 60 percent of all children's
deaths in the world are caused by hunger-related factors—an

appalling and preventable tragedy. Likewise we know that more than 800 million people are malnourished. These and so many other examples of human suffering could be rectified. On a global scale we have the resources required to do so. Already we produce enough food to ensure every person on this planet the minimum number of daily calories needed for a healthy diet. Our greatest shortcoming is a lack of collective imagination and will to make it happen. John Paul II spoke to this point directly in his encyclical On Social Concern:

> One of the greatest injustices in the contemporary world consists precisely in this: that the ones who possess much are relatively *few* and those who possess almost nothing are *many*. It is the injustice of the poor distribution of the goods and services originally intended for all. (28)

In language reminiscent of the Second Vatican Council this pontiff reminds us that the millions of people who have little or nothing "do not succeed in realizing their basic human vocation because they are deprived of essential goods" (ibid.).

We know the needs and sufferings of people throughout the world. We know the causes and we also know that we are connected to some of these causes. If we are serious about personal stewardship—about caring for the gifts and resources God has placed at our disposal—our awareness of this injustice and this human tragedy is only our first step. We must respond; we must act in practical ways. Greater knowledge and awareness call for a greater response. It calls for meaningful global stewardship.

## Helping Those Most in Need

The Judeo-Christian tradition has always demonstrated a special concern for the poor, the oppressed, the marginalized. This is seen in the Old Testament prophets admonishing the people of Israel to care for the widows, orphans, and strangers. It is seen also in the prophets' insistence on linking worship of Yahweh with acts of mercy and justice directed especially to persons who are hungry, thirsty, sick, or homeless.

This historical caring for persons with the greatest needs is reflected in Jesus' understanding of his own mission as seen in the Gospel of Luke:

> The Spirit of the Lord is upon me,
>   because he has anointed me
>     to bring good news to the poor.
> He has sent me to proclaim release to the captives
>   and recovery of sight to the blind,
>     to let the oppressed go free,
> to proclaim the year of the Lord's favor. (4:18-19)

At the conclusion of this reading Luke tells us that Jesus sat down and then said, "Today this scripture has been fulfilled in your hearing." His own ministry would be marked by special attention to the poor, the captives, the blind, the oppressed.

As we have seen throughout these chapters, early Christian theologians and church leaders never tired of reminding their readers that one of the most important acts of anyone identified as a disciple of Jesus Christ is that of reaching out to support any person who is suffering or hurting from any cause or lacking the requirements of daily living. Centuries later Catholic social documents emphasized this obligation to share our resources with those in our own society and throughout the world who are materially poor and asking for help.

These teachings remind us that the church as a body and we as individual Christians must incorporate into our mission and our lives an effective and preferential concern for the marginalized. The 1987 encyclical On Social Concern offers an example:

> By her own evangelical duty the Church feels called
> to take her stand beside the poor, to discern the justice
> of their requests, and to help satisfy them, without
> losing sight of the good of groups in the context of the
> common good. (39)

This criterion obviously governs our interaction with persons on a one-to-one basis in our own nations. But it does not end there. As John Paul II notes, it applies by analogy to international relationships, which must be transformed into solidarity and grounded in the recognition that the goods of creation are meant for all (ibid.). This standard of granting special or even preferred consideration to nations, for example, with high levels of hunger or unemployment, could guide international economic assistance efforts as well as the rules governing so many aspects of economic activity unfolding under the banner of globalization.

Within the church communities this caring for persons with greatest needs can be seen in the various programs set up by faith communities and church agencies to bring relief to the poor and to those who suffer injustice throughout the world. Among these efforts we count Catholic Charities, Lutheran Social Services, Catholic Relief Services, and Caritas International. These, and many other church-related programs, recognize the imperative necessity of reaching out to persons, groups, and communities that struggle the most to live a dignified life. The largest numbers of such needs are found beyond our national borders, a fact that begs us to practice global stewardship.

As Christians we have little choice but to engage this form of stewardship and allow our resources and talents to help bring relief and needed change to people everywhere. Early Christian writers were particularly insistent on this point. In the second century the Shepherd of Hermas asked why God allowed some Christians to be wealthy. His answer: so that these Christians might carry out for him this ministry to the poor (3.1.8-10).

John Chrysostom cautioned that mercy is essential to the Christian life but we are not really living this life when we are not showing mercy. Possession of great wealth is particularly dangerous because it can so easily undermine the virtues, the good and necessary habits, of showing compassion and mercy (*On Matthew*, Homily 52.5). On another occasion, and employing far more colorful language, this archbishop of Constantinople offered this assessment of those Christians who possess much but share little:

> I am often reproached for continually attacking the rich. Yes, because the rich are continually attacking the poor. But those I attack are not the rich as such, only those who misuse their wealth. I point out constantly that those I accuse are not the rich, but the rapacious; wealth is one thing, covetousness another. Learn to distinguish.[2]

When showing compassion and mercy to others, including those in other lands, Catholic social teaching calls us to give from our substance. Recognizing that the gifts and resources we enjoy are given to satisfy our needs and those of others, we do not hesitate to provide direct assistance where needed, and to seek changes of unjust structures that make it difficult for people in other nations to live a reasonably decent life. The guiding principle on this is the preferential option for the poor, that is, that we support those social and systemic changes that we judge will bring the greatest benefits to persons and to other nations with the greatest needs.

This preferential option for the poor appeared for the first time in Catholic social teaching with Pope Paul VI's 1971 apostolic letter, A Call to Action:

> In teaching us charity, the Gospel instructs us in the preferential respect due to the poor and the special situation they have in society: the more fortunate should renounce some of their rights so as to place their goods more generously at the service of others. (23)

Perhaps the most challenging part of this text is the Holy Father's assertion that "the more fortunate should renounce some of their rights." Though he did not elaborate on what this entails, we might draw conclusions from other teachings such as the universal purpose of the goods of creation. We may enjoy a civil, legal right to possess and enjoy all the wealth we are able to accumulate. The moral position presented by Pope Paul VI, however, tells us that we must be willing to let go of some of that wealth—renounce some of our rights—to assist other people and other nations. Voluntary contributions can be one way for this to happen as can our support of a progressive tax system.

Pope John Paul II in his 1991 encyclical, On the Hundredth Anniversary of *Rerum Novarum*, applied this principle directly to international relations and presented us with an unavoidable dimension of global stewardship. Speaking about fostering the human potential of people who are poor, the pontiff stated,

> But to accomplish this, the poor—be they individuals or nations—need to be provided with realistic opportunities. Creating such conditions calls for a concerted worldwide effort to promote development, an effort which involves sacrificing the positions of income and of power enjoyed by the more developed countries. (52)

Again, the preferential option for the poor directs us to make choices and to support those options in front of us that we believe will bring the greatest benefits to those persons and nations with the greatest needs. This is a major challenge but one we need to incorporate into our dealings with people here at home as well as those beyond our borders. It requires us to practice global stewardship in a way that bears much fruit.

The Gospel of John offers a perspective that sheds necessary light on why we must work in this way to help people meet their needs. In the context of the Good Shepherd narrative Jesus states, "I came that they may have life, and have it abundantly" (John 10:10).

The good shepherd cares for people and their needs now. He or she must not have only a "next world" orientation, lest the sheep perish in this moment. Catholic theology recognizes that the necessities of life need to be there if people are to enjoy a full, abundant, and dignified life. These necessities must be met if people anywhere are to move themselves toward that next world, however they conceive it. This too points us to practice practical and effective global stewardship.

## ✍ Getting Practical

### Loving the Neighbor We May Never Meet

Global stewardship means loving the neighbors who live beyond our borders, most of whom we likely will not have the opportunity to know. Loving the neighbor we will never meet is not impossible. It is easier today than in previous generations because our global brothers and sisters are not as removed from us as they once were. Still, by its very nature global stewardship poses challenges quite different from local stewardship. Among the many ways to address this challenge, the following seem particularly useful.

*Our Prayer Life*

The intentions within our prayers can provide a grounding for global stewardship. We pray for our own conversion, our transformation. As noted in chapter 4, our spiritual life is about responding to God's transformative presence in our lives. And so we pray that our lives will increasingly reflect the love, mercy, and compassion of Christ. If we can habitually pray for this ongoing conversion within us, we will discover how to practice global stewardship in ways that are right for us. As our hearts are changed, so too will our willingness and capacity to reach out to others beyond our nation's borders. The conversion for which we pray necessarily leads us to a different way of living, a prospect that may be frightening but exciting and fulfilling as well.

We pray also for persons actively engaged in global service or ministry. In light of the challenges and hardships they encounter in a different culture or in difficult living conditions, we pray that they may have the fortitude and courage to continue. We pray that the example of their loving service may continue to inspire the rest of us to recognize and act on our solidarity with people everywhere, especially those whose needs we may be in a position to alleviate.

Our prayer intentions may include specific persons, groups, and communities whose particular situation touches us. This often happens with people who go on mission trips. They are so moved by a community or family they came to know in another country that this family becomes one of their prayer intentions on into the future. However, when we pray for somebody or some cause, our prayer should move us to action. That is, what we pray for is what we should help become a reality. If we pray for a family we met on a trip to Guatemala, perhaps there is a concrete action we can take to help meet that family's needs. Our prayer is that God will bless this family with his love and care, but also that we do what is within our ability to help meet its needs. That may be why we were endowed with particular resources—to perform God's ministry to the poor for him, as the Shepherd of Hermas states. In any case, we must always remember that what we pray for is what we should help bring about.

### Our Actions

Our contributions of money and material goods is a good starting point for engaging in global stewardship. Making donations is practical and it is something that most of us can do at some level. Even if our contributions are quite small, they are important because they provide needed assistance to someone else, and because they offer the potential to draw us more deeply into acts of global stewardship, acts that can transform us in ways not expected.

We might support organizations or projects involved in global poverty, development, and peace—particularly those that align with our interests and passions. If these carry the opportunity to have contact with people being served by the program, the potential for our own education and conversion to new ways of seeing the world is without limit. My own two-year experience as a Peace Corps volunteer in Turkey leaves me convinced that having relationships with people in another country can open a very large door to global stewardship. After many decades, I no longer have contact with the residents of Yenişehir, but the benefits from that experience of living in another country among people of a different culture and religion have never ended.

### Our Advocacy

Working for needed changes in present programs, institutions, and structures—advocating for more just social systems—is also a form of stewardship. Using our gifts to help bring change and empower people in other nations is one of the most important expressions of global stewardship.

This may take the form of direct humanitarian relief, like advocating for affordable medications to treat persons in parts of Africa afflicted with HIV/AIDS. It may also involve advocating for changes in our own nation's economic policies as they impact poorer countries. One example would be to increase support for international food aid and, especially in the Food for Peace funding, to make it possible for small farmers in developing nations to grow more of their own food. Other efforts may include general trade agreements, or the subsidizing of US agricultural commodities to the detriment of small farmers in Mexico or India, or support for fair-trade policies and programs. Another example could be to support programs like Catholics Confront Global Poverty, an initiative of Catholic Relief Services and the United States Conference of Catholic Bishops aimed at educating US Catholics and advocating for poverty-focused international assistance.

We may become involved in advocating for new ways of thinking about development and peace. This may include promoting the teaching of Pope Paul VI that development is the way to peace. Advocacy may combine with education to promote the benefits of solidarity and living the preferential option for the poor as well as sharing with food deficit nations the needed resources and technology. Our advocacy can advance the claim that all of this is a much neglected road to inter-national development and a far surer path to global peace than continued American military intervention.

## Notes

1. John Chrysostom, *Homily 2 on Lazarus*, in *On Wealth and Poverty*, trans. Catharine P. Roth (Crestwood, NY: St. Vladimir's Seminary Press, 1984), 49.

2. John Chrysostom, *Fall of Eutropius* 2.3, quoted in William J. Walsh and John P. Langan, "Patristic Social Consciousness—The Church and the Poor," *The Faith That Does Justice: Examining the Christian Sources for Social Change*, ed. John C. Haughey, Woodstock Studies 2 (New York: Paulist, 1977), 128.

# 8

# Ecological Stewardship

Faithfulness will spring up from the ground,
     and righteousness will look down from the sky.
The LORD will give what is good,
     and our land will yield its increase.

—Psalm 85:11-12

Stewardship means caring for something that belongs to another. As Christians we see this as taking care of what belongs to God, and that includes our looking after all of creation. As applied to the material world this sense of stewardship means more than a simple, unattached "watching over." It also suggests that we love and deeply appreciate the glory surrounding this beautiful world that we protect, a point repeated in several of the Hebrew psalms.

O LORD, how manifold are your works!
     In wisdom you have made them all;
          the earth is full of your creatures. (Ps 104:24)

The psalmist marvels at all that God has created: the waters, clouds, and winds; mountains and valleys; gentle streams that nourish wild animals and birds; grass and plants to feed cattle and people (and wine to gladden human hearts); even the young roaring lions seek their food from God. All creatures look to God for sustenance, to the Creator who continually renews the face of the earth.

It is difficult to find a better appreciation of ecological stewardship than that expressed in various psalms. In these psalms we see a recognition that everything owes its creation and sustenance to God. There too, we see an appreciation of how it all works together—and a call for all living things, including humans, to sing to God and to rejoice in this wondrous world our Creator has fashioned.

So why include ecology in a discussion of stewardship? What does environmental ethics have to do with our definition of stewardship: caring for what belongs to another? Why should we care for the earth and all the creatures living here? From a biblical standpoint we find several answers to this question. We care for the earth—and the entire universe (creation)—because it is God's, because it is good, because God asks us to care for it, and because we need it.

### It Is God's

Our starting point for practicing stewardship of creation is the simple recognition that all of it belongs to God:

> The earth is the Lord's and all that is in it,
>     the world, and those who live in it. (Ps 24:1)

It is difficult to find a reason for why we should practice this form of stewardship that is clearer and more direct than this verse from Psalm 24. We are living in and using a world that belongs to God. Whatever we use for our sustenance, we owe an acknowledgment of gratitude to God who provided it.

In the first creation story we read that God gave humans what they need for food:

> God said, "See, I have given you every plant yielding seed that is upon the face of the earth, and every tree with seed in its fruit; you shall have them for food. (Gen 1:29)

Later in chapter 9, after the great flood, God offers humans other sources of food: "Every moving thing that lives shall be food for you; and just as I gave you the green plants, I give you everything" (9:3).

The point of these texts is not to provide material for debating whether humans should be vegetarians, but to appreciate that everything we have to sustain our lives has been given to us by God, by the one owner of all these life-supporting goods. In daily living we all know that we normally don't give to another person something that is not ours. If we choose to share our money or food or clothing with somebody else, we are sharing what we consider to be ours. We don't express our generosity by giving what belongs to another person. The Genesis texts that have God providing us with food follows that same pattern. God gives us what is his; we are able to eat and survive in every way because God generously provides for us out of his creation.

In our grace before meals we offer a small expression of gratitude to the Creator who made it possible for someone to grow or produce this food that "we are about to receive from your bounty." The same is true for all that we take from nature to provide for a comfortable living—trees for the wood to build our homes; iron ore to make steel for constructing office buildings, cars, and trains; water to allow us to function. All of these are available to us as gifts from the one who owns them: the Creator of the universe.

In chapter 1 we developed more fully this theme that all of creation belongs to God. Obviously that includes nature and all that comes to mind when we talk about the environment and ecology. It is especially in this world—in nature—that we can appreciate "God's creation" and why we must practice ecological stewardship.

## It Is Good

We care for creation also because it is good, and our use of any part of it must not diminish its inherent beauty and worth. This goodness of creation comes not from its usefulness to humans, but from its being created by God. In the first creation story in the book of Genesis, at the end of each day God looks upon what he has created and sees that it is good (1:4, 10, 12, 18, 21, 25). All creation is deemed good even before humans are on the scene.

This is a point worth keeping before us in light of our tendency through history to regard the rest of creation as having value only insofar as it can please or in some way benefit humans. The long-standing practice of using animals for testing cosmetic products seems to rest on that kind of thinking. So did the nineteenth- and twentieth-century practice of draining "swamps" (wetlands) so that farmers could make productive use of that land by growing corn or other crops. Certainly ecological stewardship allows us to work with the natural setting, even to make alterations that can serve human needs. At issue, however, is the attitude we have toward nature and the role we set for ourselves when we decide to make such changes. Everything in God's creation has value and purpose, and our limited ability to recognize that should not diminish the importance of this claim.

This recognition of the intrinsic value of creation is highlighted in the United States Catholic bishops' 1991 pastoral statement on the environment, Renewing the Earth:

> Accordingly, it is appropriate that we treat other creatures and the natural world not just as means to human fulfillment but also as God's creatures, possessing an independent value, worthy of our respect and care. (7)

A year earlier in his 1990 World Day of Peace message Pope John Paul II made an interesting connection between this teaching and the traditional Catholic emphasis upon respect for life. Near the end of this document he specifically addresses "my Catholic brothers and sisters"—we who strongly champion respect for life and the right to life for humans. The Holy Father tells us to include all of creation in that life:

> Respect for life and for the dignity of the human person extends also to the rest of creation, which is called

to join us in praising God (cf. Ps. 148 and 96). (The
Ecological Crisis: A Common Responsibility 16)

The respect we show for human life and for the dignity of the
human person must be shown also to the rest of creation: because it is God's, because it is good, because it also is called
to praise God. Here we might recall from chapter 1 the sabbatical laws that point to the land and all of creation—not just
humans—enjoying a relationship with God. At the very least
we might humbly reflect, with the psalms in front of us, on
how the sun and moon and stars are able to praise the Lord,
as are the mountains, hills, fruit trees, cedars, along with wild
animals and cattle, creeping things, and birds (Ps 148). Ecological stewardship calls us to see that every bit of creation
has value and every bit of this value comes from the Creator.

Renewing the Earth speaks of this good creation as sacramental—the whole universe is God's dwelling: "Through
the created gifts of nature, men and women encounter their
Creator" (6). God is present to us through all of creation, and
through the manifold works of God we are able to find peace
and comfort in the presence of our Creator. This is the language of sacraments, meeting God through rituals involving
ordinary materials of life. What a remarkably "Catholic" way
to appreciate the goodness of creation! The bishops point to
where this may lead:

> The Christian vision of a sacramental universe—a
> world that discloses the Creator's presence by visi-
> ble and tangible signs—can contribute to making the
> earth a home for the human family once again. (Re-
> newing the Earth 6)

At a time when we live with the fear of climate change and
its consequences in such phenomena as rising sea levels and
more severe weather events, this is a hopeful message. The
universe is sacramental. It too is a privileged place for experiencing our God. In gratitude we acknowledge that we
are participants in this amazing work of God: "then the Lord

God formed man from the dust of the ground . . . Out of the ground the LORD God made to grow every tree . . . every animal of the field and every bird of the air (Gen 2:7, 9, 19).

We humans are made of the same stuff as the trees, animals, and birds. We are connected to the rest of creation. We are part of this creation that God looked upon and said, "It is good."

## God Expects Us to Care for Creation

We practice ecological stewardship also because this is what God asks us to do. Caring for creation is an expectation that flows from our relationship with God. Humans, of all created beings, are given a particular responsibility for the rest of creation.

As noted in chapter 1, the first creation story speaks of humans being given dominion over the rest of creation. Too often this dominion has been interpreted to suggest humans are sole rulers of the earth and have authority to do whatever they wish with the natural world. Biblical scholars, however, advise that this "dominion" is to be a form of ruling in the place of God, as God would, with compassion and love and justice.

Catholic social teachings on this topic have not been as clear or nuanced as we might hope or even expect. Until very recently the major documents, including those of the Second Vatican Council, speak of humans dominating. The Pastoral Constitution on the Church in the Modern World declared, "Men and women were created in God's image and were commanded to conquer the earth with all it contains and to rule the world in justice and holiness" (34). John Paul II, as noted earlier in this chapter, called us to extend respect for life and the dignity of the human person to the rest of creation. Yet he too in his great encyclical On Human Work writes of humans "dominating the earth" and "subduing the earth" in ways reminiscent of Americans in past generations using the language of "conquering the Wild West."

Clearly these social teachings did not intend to promote any kind of activity or behavior harmful to the environment or to any aspect of God's good creation. Wherever the language of "dominating" or "subduing" is found, the broader context makes it quite clear that the papal or council writers were proposing a human presence within nature that ultimately honors the Creator. Still, the use of this vocabulary in such unnuanced ways reflects a bit of the ambiguity that has accompanied humankind's march through history, and through the natural world.

A more recent and hopeful comment on this subject comes in the US Catholic bishops' Renewing the Earth:

> Stewardship implies that we must both care for creation according to the standards that are not of our own making and at the same time be resourceful in finding ways to make it flourish. It is a difficult balance, requiring both a sense of limits and a spirit of experimentation. (6)

In more recent decades official Catholic documents tend to acknowledge this dual role and responsibility that humans have for the rest of creation. On the one hand, we are to protect and care for the earth; on the other, we should use our God-given intelligence and creativity to help the earth to flourish. At times this responsibility takes on the language of "co-creators" (Renewing the Earth 12), where it can mean caring for creation and making needed changes to ensure that the natural world will be in a position to satisfy human needs of today and those in the distant future.

Returning to the book of Genesis, men and women have no choice but to be stewards of this good creation that is God's. The second creation story, which reminds us of our connectedness to the rest of creation, offers the wonderful image of caring for the garden: "The Lord God took the man and put him in the garden of Eden to till it and keep it" (Gen 2:15). This garden image can easily be expanded to caring for the earth—our garden, our residence, our source of all we need. Surely we may use what we find in this garden to meet our needs and those of our neighbors. God gave it for that purpose.

But our use of the goods of creation must respect the needs of all other creatures in the garden. While using creation we must keep it in good condition because it is God's, because it is good, because others—now and in the future, human and non-human—also need it. Indeed, humans do have a special role in caring for the garden. We are stewards of God's creation.

## Because We Need It

Of all the reasons given for why we should practice ecological stewardship, none is more self-evident and immediate than the simple truth that our lives depend upon the natural world and the environment that surrounds us. We need the rest of creation far more than it needs us, and we need it to be in a healthy condition. Our survival and that of our sisters and brothers in coming generations is dependent upon the air, water, soil, and all life forms that we so casually take for granted.

Not only humans but all other species in God's creation require a stable environment able to provide minimal levels of food, water, and shelter. Scientists studying the effects of human-induced climate change already note that some species are adapting while others may perish before they are able to make the necessary adjustments. All living creatures, including humans, need a habitable environment—one that God provides within creation, but one that may be threatened by the excesses of human behavior.

One of the lessons that the human species is slow to learn is the interconnectedness of everything on this planet. In so many ways we pollute the air or contaminate water sources with little thought to the disastrous consequences that follow. This is the pattern of behavior behind climate change or ground water contamination or the elimination of habitat for various species. Our shortsighted and sometimes selfish choices may result in suffering for future generations of humans as well as other species.

In 2001 the US Catholic bishops gave us a pastoral statement on this topic, Global Climate Change: A Plea for Dialogue,

Prudence, and the Common Good. They made the argument that even when some uncertainty remains regarding the extent and causes of climate change, our response to this phenomenon must be "rooted in the virtue of prudence" (2). Though we may not be 100 percent certain that humans are causing climate change or that sea levels will rise to extremely dangerous levels, prudence bids us to err on the side of caution. We have a moral obligation to take precautions now to lessen the likelihood of these catastrophes visiting our children and grandchildren. We today do not have a moral right to act in ways that place future generations at risk.

The earth is here for our use, but this use should be of a manner that neither destroys nor depletes, a use that is tempered by a loving concern for those who come after us. John Paul II, with his emphasis on solidarity, stressed that this responsibility for others extended beyond our own lifetimes:

> [W]e cannot interfere in one area of the ecosystem without paying due attention both to the consequences of such interference in other areas and to the well-being of future generations. (The Ecological Crisis: A Common Responsibility 6)

His statement reflects the very nature of ecology as a scientific discipline, that is, that we continually learn how closely connected everything is—that actions in one place affect life elsewhere, that our choices today carry consequences that many generations after us will have to confront.

The impact of human behavior on the rest of creation is recognized throughout the Sacred Scriptures. The negative effects of human misconduct are presented with dreadful detail by the prophet Hosea:

> Hear the word of the LORD, O people of Israel;
>> for the LORD has an indictment against the inhabitants
>>> of the land.
> There is no faithfulness or loyalty,
>> and no knowledge of God in the land.

> Swearing, lying, and murder,
>> and stealing and adultery break out;
>> bloodshed follows bloodshed.
> Therefore the land mourns,
>> and all who live in it languish;
> together with the wild animals
>> and the birds of the air,
>> even the fish of the sea are perishing. (4:1-3)

The earth always suffers from direct human mistreatment, such as polluting lakes and rivers or farming in ways that cause soil to erode. Hosea, however, is making an argument that how we live on a daily basis in our dealings with God and with one another also affects how well or poorly the natural world does. Our failure to live in right relationship with God (no faithfulness or loyalty, or knowledge of God) results in suffering for all creation. So does our failure to live in right relationship with one another (swearing, lying, murder, stealing, adultery). This is what John Paul II may have had in mind when he wrote that the ecological crisis is fundamentally a moral crisis "of which the destruction of the environment is only one troubling aspect" (Ecological Crisis 5). Our failure to walk in God's way, to live in justice and peace with God and with our brothers and sisters, inevitably leads to suffering for the rest of creation, and ultimately to our own hurt for we cause the destruction of what we need for survival.

On the other hand, when we learn to "walk in the light of the Lord" as described in the messianic texts of Isaiah, there will be no more training for war (Isa 2:2-5) and all creatures will recline as one together in the peaceable kingdom (Isa 11:6-9). Then, too, the earth—which we need—will flourish.

> Steadfast love and faithfulness will meet;
>> righteousness and peace will kiss each other.
> Faithfulness will spring up from the ground,
>> and righteousness will look down from the sky.
> The LORD will give what is good,
>> and our land will yield its increase. (Ps 85:10-12)

When we live in faithfulness to God's laws, to the expectations of our relationship with God, then the rest of creation is at peace. When we live in harmony with one another, then the land itself will increase its yield. Harmony, peace, and joy-filled hope are the fruits of our practicing ecological stewardship.

## ✍ Getting Practical

### Checking Lifestyles and Embracing Environmental Justice

Ecological stewardship engages us on many levels because the biblical command to care for what is God's touches every area of our lives. This form of stewardship especially draws from the biblical understanding of justice, living out the expectations of our many relationships. To live in this practical manner, three suggestions seem appropriate.

*Examine and Change Our Lifestyle*

We may begin by asking whether our own lifestyle may be contributing to unnecessary stress upon the environment. This recognizes that there may be a few fairly obvious and relatively painless ways in which we can change daily practices or routines to show greater respect and care for God's creation. Are we wasteful with the water we use? Do we drive our cars for very short errands where walking is an alternative? Does our shopping and purchasing in the area of wants go beyond what is consistent with a position of concern for the environment?

In their 1991 pastoral statement on the environment the US Catholic bishops stated that consumption is the single greatest threat to the environment. In what ways do our patterns of consumption contribute to this problem? What concrete changes can we make in how we live? What practical options do we have? Pressing this a bit further, we might ask, What sacrifices are we willing to make? To guide us in all of this we should ask how our faith shapes the way we answer these questions. What importance do we give to the values suggested by our religious tradition?

One very practical step we may consider is to take the St. Francis Pledge to Care for Creation and the Poor. This is a promise and a commitment to live our faith by protecting God's creation and advocating on behalf of people in poverty—the ones who face the harshest impacts of environmental degradation (www.catholicclimatecovenant.org).

### Educate and Advocate about the Environment

Beyond examining our own lives, we can help others to understand more clearly the need for all of us to make changes in the way we live. An effective way to do this is through our local parish or congregation. Many of our parishes support some kind of social ministry work, an effort often led by a committee of persons particularly interested in social justice issues. This could be the place to see if our parish is doing anything about educating parishioners regarding their church's teachings on the environment.

We might connect also with other programs and organizations that advocate for public policy changes that can benefit land, water, and natural habitat for other species. One example of this could be the US farm bill that is renewed every five years. This piece of legislation determines much of federal support for conservation programs related to farming. A helpful place to learn about this is the National Catholic Rural Life Conference (www.ncrlc.com).

Do we know what other programs and organizations are out there advocating for changes that can benefit the environment? Do we know what already is being done? The point here is that we need not and should not try to engage in advocacy by ourselves. The most effective way to use our gifts in this area is to join with or at least support others who already are working on issues that especially hold our interests. Always it is important to focus upon efforts that work from a values system consistent with our own faith.

*Educate and Advocate about Environmental Justice*

Our concern about caring for God's creation is a concern both for the natural environment and for people. It can never be one or the other. Within this approach we recognize that environmental degradation brings the greatest hardship to persons and communities with limited resources. These are especially communities marked by high levels of poverty, people least able to avoid or mitigate the harsh effects of natural or human-caused disasters. And, they are least able to respond.

The Carteret islanders are a contemporary representation of this truth. They live on a small island fifty miles off the coast of Bougainville, a province of Papua New Guinea. These islanders are now forced to move and find a new homeland because the sea is rising up, already spreading saltwater over their fertile farmland and destroying their ability to grow the food upon which their survival depends. They are climate change's earliest refugees. Their story is told in a documentary film, *Sun Come Up*. It is brief, clear, and well worth viewing.

We might become familiar with programs that seek to address the many consequences of environmental problems in areas populated by low-income and minority groups. Likewise we can find direction with organizations working to prevent the placement of environmentally harmful facilities in these same areas. A starting point for all of this is to connect our local church efforts with any denominational effort to address human suffering caused by environmental problems. Within the Catholic Church a good example of this is the Environmental Justice Program sponsored by the US Conference of Catholic Bishops (http://www.usccb.org/issues-and-action/human-life-and-dignity/environment/environmental-justice-program/).

# 9

# Financial Stewardship

Then he called his disciples and said to them, "Truly I tell you, this poor widow has put in more than all those who are contributing to the treasury. For all of them have contributed out of their abundance; but she out of her poverty has put in everything she had, all she had to live on."

—Mark 12:43-44

Stewardship is caring for what belongs to God. It is rooted in a recognition that everything we have is from God and everything we have is God's. Christian discipleship guides us to use our material resources and our innate talents with that in mind. There are many ways to talk about stewardship just as there are many ways to practice it—global, local, ecological, personal.

Another form of stewardship, and perhaps the most commonly understood one, is financial. When people hear the term "stewardship" in the context of the parish or congregation, they most likely think of financial support. Even when organizers of "Stewardship Sunday" insist that this refers to time, talents, and treasures, it is likely that a majority of the listeners in the pews are thinking this is mostly about treasures, that is, monetary contributions.

Financial stewardship may be a way of practicing the other forms of stewardship. Contributing money can be a practical and sometimes easy way to engage in acts of charity or advocacy or simply supporting our church. This can be problematic if we become accustomed to providing financial support without engaging ourselves in ways that not only help the recipient of our contributions but also lead to our own conversion and transformation. On the other hand, with proper motivation such financial stewardship can become a profound act of gratitude to our Creator and a proclamation that the reign of God is at hand.

### Express Gratitude

Financial stewardship proceeds from a grateful recognition that all we have is a gift, that all we possess and enjoy has been given. If we have difficulty accepting this claim, we might ask ourselves, Why am I doing well and others aren't? Why was I born into this family with supportive and healthy ties when some of my classmates or coworkers struggle to live balanced, happy lives in homes with broken relationships? Why do I live here and not in some country burdened by civil war or awash in natural disasters?

At times we are tempted to think, I worked hard for what I have. I earned it, and my earnings are not someone else's entitlement. It is at such moments that we should ask ourselves, From where or from whom did I receive the skills and abilities to do so well? Who gave me the energy, ambition, and work ethic so necessary for my success?

None of us are self-made individuals. We did not create ourselves. The same God who made rain fall on the just and the unjust (Matt 5:45) is the God who sees some people struggle through a life of recurring illnesses and poverty while others flourish in economic and social well-being. We may not understand why this is so, but we need to recognize that it is so. Our success in life has much to do with the Creator allowing us to be born in this society or family and with these particular talents, passions, and drives.

In spite of cultural messages about one person or another being a self-made success story, none of us created ourselves.

We need to be clear about the source of our good fortunes, just as we need to acknowledge that the misfortune and suffering of so many people in our world is not because God wants this, but because we humans allow it to continue. If we can do that, then we likewise can benefit from reflecting on why the Christian is expected to share his or her financial resources. Saint Paul's second letter to the Corinthians is helpful:

> You will be enriched in every way for your great generosity, which will produce thanksgiving to God through us; for the rendering of this ministry not only supplies the needs of the saints but also overflows with many thanksgivings to God. (2 Cor 9:11-12)

The blessings we already enjoy, the good things we possess—our riches—are given so that we may be generous. The message from St. Paul is not primarily that we will be blessed if we are generous. Rather, the point is that we must be generous in thanksgiving for the many blessings already received. Our generosity then will lead others, especially the recipients, to thank God who is the source of every good. It is this God who moves us to be charitable in the distribution of our resources. Will we in turn be rewarded for our generosity? Perhaps, but the focus here is on God, the bestower of all that is good and the one who has put us into a position to be generous.

Homilies or talks during financial stewardship campaigns occasionally seek to assure listeners that blessings will come their way if they give generously. They have it backwards. We should give generously because we already have been blessed by a loving God. There is nothing wrong with believing that our generosity will be rewarded by God but that should not be the motivation for our giving. We give out of grateful hearts because God has blessed us already and we want our act of sharing to give glory to God.

If we are generous, others will praise God for what they receive. They will thank God for the generosity of those who give and make it possible for them to eat and live in security.

The poor of Chimbote, Peru, praise God each morning for generous benefactors who contribute to their needs. Certainly they are praying for their benefactors, but their prayer fundamentally is one of praise to God who inspires this generosity in people living on different continents. These morning prayers in the Church of Our Lady of Perpetual Help remind us of a teaching from the early Christian writers, that the poor can be our best advocates before God as well as our greatest accusers: "the Lord beholds what is done toward them, and every deed cries louder than a herald to him who searches all hearts."[1] Another Christian theologian in the second century, Tertullian, stated this point in even more powerful language: the sufferer's grateful prayers to God for his benefactor are in effect the prayers of Christ (*Prescription Against Heretics* 20).

Some years back a pastoral letter from the Archdiocese of Los Angeles summed up this idea that financial stewardship is an expression of gratitude for what we already have received:

> The whole of the Christian life is a response to a gift received. Our call is to live from a grateful heart. (For This You Were Called, "I. Learning How to Receive")

Our life is to reflect our awareness of what has happened to us through Christ. Our daily living is an unbroken continuation of our eucharistic celebration, an expression of gratitude for being restored to right relationship with God, with our neighbor, and with all of creation.

This gratitude for what has happened to us through the life, death, and resurrection of Jesus Christ takes the form of practical and generous responses to needs within our world and within our church. It is about living with a spirit of generosity, one that is formed in a grateful heart.

## Proclaim the Reign of God

To live from this posture of gratitude is to proclaim the reign of God. It is to live as though something new is upon us. It is to live in a way that causes others to notice that values different from those of popular culture are guiding our lives. Such living rises from our core convictions that the Gospel call to turn to God and to love our neighbor means that our daily lives must be different, that an entirely new era has dawned as we read in the Gospel of Mark:

> Now after John was arrested, Jesus came to Galilee, proclaiming the good news of God, and saying, "The time is fulfilled, and the kingdom of God has come near; repent, and believe in the good news." (1:14-15)

Jesus announces the nearness of the kingdom of God and then proclaims what an appropriate response on our part would look like: repent, undergo a conversion, respond to God's presence in your life. Most important, believe this good news, and let your lives be a witness to this belief.

There are many ways for us to express these convictions throughout our lives. One is by exhibiting gratitude, love, and compassion in all of our relationships and in each of our choices and actions. We do this also by providing resources to programs and organizations that work to enrich everyone's lives and build a more compassionate world. These are efforts that endeavor to bring closer the kind of world compatible with the full realization of the reign of God. In gratitude for Jesus' saving message that this reign of God is near, we support those whose mission it is to continue this joy-filled proclamation.

Financial stewardship is about providing such resources. It allows us to use the resources with which we have been gifted and to do so in that gratefully loving and compassionate way so reflective of the ministry of Jesus of Nazareth. Thus do we witness that something new is upon us—that the reign of God has begun in our hearts, in our lives, in our world. Financial stewardship is a practical way for us to support the organized efforts of the church—locally, regionally, globally—to preach God's word, to proclaim the reign of God.

## Share from Our Substance

When making contributions to any cause, there always is the question of how much we should consider giving. Difficult as it may be to hear, financial stewardship is not giving from our leftover resources after all our needs and wants are met. Rather, it is about making our resources available—it is about sharing from our substance. The book of Deuteronomy points to why we give and one of the uses to which those donations should be directed:

> Set apart a tithe of all the yield of your seed that is brought in yearly from the field. (14:22)

As we discussed in chapter 1, our offering or tithe is a simple but direct acknowledgment that this harvest, this produce—these financial resources upon which our lives depend—are in our keeping because of God. Our offering becomes a reminder for us that these resources we possess ultimately come from and belong to God.

> Every third year you shall bring out the full tithe of your produce for that year, and store it within your towns; the Levites, because they have no allotment or inheritance with you, as well as the resident aliens, the orphans, and the widows in your towns, may come and eat their fill so that the Lord your God may bless you in all the work that you undertake. (Deut 14:28-29)

The peoples' offering of the tithe is given to members of the community who have obvious needs—those who minister in the temple, the widows, the orphans, and the strangers. The Israelites are well aware that their relationship with God is connected to their relationship with one another, especially to those in their midst who lack needed resources. The offering of the tithe and its designated use among the marginalized points to that relationship. In the very act of providing for their livelihood (harvesting produce from the land) the people honor their relationship with God through the offering of the tithe, which becomes sustenance for the poor and marginalized in their midst. This is proclaiming the reign of God. It is giving flesh to their hope and their conviction that God is with them. It is providing a witness to the fact that life has been changed, that a different set of values now guides their decisions, that accumulating as much wealth and material possessions as possible is not life's highest goal.

Financial stewardship means giving from our substance. Jesus offers a beautiful example of this as recounted in Mark's gospel:

> [Jesus] sat down opposite the treasury, and watched the crowd putting money into the treasury. Many rich people put in large sums. A poor widow came and put in two small copper coins, which are worth a penny. Then he called his disciples and said to them, "Truly I tell you, this poor widow has put in more than all those who are contributing to the treasury. For all of them have contributed out of their abundance; but she out of her poverty has put in everything she had, all she had to live on." (Mark 12:41-44)

Some years ago the people in Fr. Jack Davis's parish in Chimbote, Peru, relived this parable. For many decades they had received much money from people throughout the world, especially from communities in North Dakota, the home area of their pastor. So in 1997 when they heard about the devastating flood in and around Grand Forks, North Dakota, they thought it was they who must now give. Their city's main industry is canning fish—mostly anchovies and sardines harvested in the Pacific Ocean off the northern coast of Peru. So, they decided to send two cartons of sardines to the people of Grand Forks who had lost so much to the unstoppable flooding of the Red River of the North. On hearing this, Fr. Jack wondered what good will a few dozen cans of sardines do for the thousands of people suffering in Grand Forks. Then he remembered the poor widow and her two little copper coins.

Financial stewardship means giving from our substance, whether that is the wealth of a pauper or of a millionaire. This point is grounded in the earliest theology within Christianity, and repeated in modern Catholic social teachings:

> Therefore everyone has the right to possess a sufficient amount of the earth's goods for themselves and their family. This has been the opinion of the Fathers and Doctors of the church, who taught that people are bound to come to the aid of the poor and to do so not merely out of their superfluous goods. (Church in the Modern World 69 [see n. 10])

Giving from our substance should be the standard. This does not mean putting ourselves into economic poverty, but responding to others' needs from the abundance of riches we have received or developed. St. Paul urges the earliest Christians to give generously without fear of impoverishment:

> Each of you must give as you have made up your mind, not reluctantly or under compulsion, for God loves a cheerful giver. And God is able to provide you with every blessing in abundance, so that by always having enough of everything, you may share abundantly in every good work. (2 Cor 9:7-8)

Paul's reassuring message is that God will not allow us to slip into poverty simply because we are generous in our giving. We always will have enough of what we need. Fear of not having enough for ourselves should never prevent us from giving generously. Having enough, for New Testament writers, typically meant being content with basics, like food and clothing. The writer of 1 Timothy presents the danger with wanting to possess and hold on to more:

> But those who want to be rich fall into temptation and are trapped by many senseless and harmful desires that plunge people into ruin and destruction. For the love

> of money is a root of all kinds of evil, and in their ea-
> gerness to be rich some have wandered away from the
> faith and pierced themselves with many pains. (6:9-10)

The desire to be rich can lead us "away from the faith" and
trap us in distorted visions of what is required to live as followers of Jesus Christ. Most immediately, an obsession with
riches can cloud our grasp of how we should see our possessions in relation to our sisters and brothers, our communities,
and our church. Too often the "ruin and destruction" that
come with a passion for wealth includes a loss of memory
regarding who ultimately is the owner of the possessions we
call "ours," and what will happen to them at the moment of
our death. The writer of 1 Timothy continues this discussion
by noting that we brought nothing into the world, so we can
take nothing out of it.

Jesus' teaching on giving to the temple and our reflection
on giving to our church should not be divorced from the related message in Deuteronomy. There is a connection between
making a financial contribution to the temple (church) and
the use of that collection in ministering to the poor. As active
parishioners contributing to our local church, we should be
clear about that connection and make sure that our parish is
using our contributions accordingly.

## Join Ecclesial Efforts

Financial stewardship for most people means giving to the
church. That may be an accurate statement but it hardly cap-
tures the depth and breadth of what this form of stewardship
represents. If by "giving to the church" we mean contributing
to the maintenance of the parish buildings, that is partially
correct. But there is much more that we are asked to support.
We may look upon this form of giving as helping to pay the
salaries of parish leaders and employees—pastor, liturgy director, administrator, faith formation director, social ministry
coordinator, and more. Again, this is not a mistaken way of
understanding financial stewardship; it is just not complete.

There is a tendency for many Catholics to view their financial contributions as fulfilling their obligations to support their parish's mission and various ministries. Truly the money is important, but equally important is the parishioner's active involvement in the life of the parish, for the sake of both the parish and the parishioner. God has given every one of us talents and skills that can be used for carrying out our parish's ministries through volunteering or simply participating in the many programs the parish offers.

Over the past couple of decades sociologists and anthropologists have noted the increasing reluctance of Americans to join social groups and commit to regular participation. We are far more likely to send a check to an organization we like than to become a member and make a commitment of our time, and this includes parish and other church-related activities. The classic example of this trend—and the title of a book on this topic—is the fact that more and more Americans are bowling but not joining bowling leagues. We are bowling alone.

Clearly this trend poses problems, especially as it relates to financial stewardship and our parish. If all we do is write a check and perhaps attend Sunday Mass, we are depriving ourselves and our parish of so much more we could offer. Participating in weekly liturgy is very important for many and obvious reasons. If that worship, however, does not lead us to other forms of engagement within our faith community, we risk having Sunday Mass become a personally satisfying experience but lacking in the communal dimension of public worship and, more broadly, what church membership requires of us.

All the forms of stewardship we discussed come together in our active involvement in local church. There we find articulated the reasons for developing our gifts and placing them at the service of the church and the world. There too, at least in a thriving parish, are the opportunities for practicing all forms of stewardship: local, global, ecological, personal. Within the liturgical and educational life of our local church we hear again and again the foundational theological reasons for practicing stewardship—recognizing that all of creation is God's, caring for God's people, and living in just relationships.

Financial stewardship should draw us into this rich and transforming life within our parish. A monetary contribution can be so much more than "paying someone else" to do the work of the church that baptism empowers all of us to do. We need to follow the money and become active in some of the programs our financial gift supports. As with prayer, we not only pray or pay for something to happen; we also become involved with our many gifts and expertise as a way of increasing the chances of it happening. To do so enriches the parish and provides us with multiple opportunities for conversion.

Financial stewardship is one of the easiest ways for us to help our parish as well as our diocese and the universal church to carry out its mission. On the parish level, most mission statements speak of this faith community as rooted in the Gospel of Jesus Christ, and committed to the spiritual growth and social well-being of its members.

Every parish has the goals of (1) proclaiming the Gospel through preaching, religious education, and active witness; (2) celebrating the presence of God through liturgical and sacramental life; (3) forming and nurturing a local faith community; and (4) reaching out in service and justice to the larger society and world. Financial stewardship makes it possible for our parish to live these goals and to carry out its mission. Never should we lose sight of these goals—however they may be worded—and never should we as a faith community compromise our mission by a reluctance either to provide adequate financial resources or to offer our own time and talents to the realization of that mission.

We the baptized are responsible for realizing the mission of the church, but this is something we do in concert with the entire ecclesial body. Our relationship with God, our formation as disciples of Jesus Christ, is tied up with this mission. We require help to do this; we need the support of our faith community. Our theology reminds us of this unavoidable communal dimension to living the Gospel of Jesus Christ. It may be alright to go bowling alone, but our journey to God is best done in the company of the people of God.

# ✍ Getting Practical

## Joining Parish Efforts

Financial stewardship is one form or one part of the general stewardship we are called to live. Stewardship as a way of life provides the necessary context for practicing financial stewardship. Among the many practices likely to encourage sound financial stewardship, three merit particular attention.

### *Develop All of Our Gifts and Resources*

As we saw in the discussion of the parable of the Talents (Matt 25:14-30), we must develop the gifts we have received. All of these talents and resources have been given for a purpose larger than our own comfort. It is not wrong to do well financially, but we need to hold the right perspective regarding our talents and skills and especially regarding whatever material wealth and possessions we are fortunate to possess.

That perspective will keep us clear on how we made it to where we are. It also will not allow us to forget who endowed us with the abilities to do as well as we do, including our enjoyment of whatever financial success we may achieve. Additionally, this perspective will guide us in using our abundance in the best possible manner—for ourselves and our dependents, for the various communities in which we participate, for whatever parish, congregation, or faith community we join, and for those persons who lack needed resources and abilities. In this outlook there is much room for a humble appreciation of the many gifts with which God has blessed us and made it possible for us to do well. That appreciation is best demonstrated by an unending spirit of generosity on our part.

### *Commit to Lifelong Learning*

Ongoing reflection, study, and learning are the surest ways to appreciate what all of this means for each of us. Our lives are constantly changing. As we grow and mature into adulthood

and beyond, we hope that our accomplishments and material
well-being grow with us. Whatever attitudes we had about success and wealth as a fifteen-year-old may not serve us well as we
move into our thirties or fifties or seventies. As we change, so
must our appreciation of where we stand in our communities,
churches, and social circles. That calls for lifelong reflection,
study, and learning.

We might draw a lesson from the early church. As membership in the Christian church grew during the third and fourth
centuries, there were more and more people of wealth joining
the faithful. This led to early church writers like St. Ambrose
reflecting and writing on the responsibilities of the rich toward
persons living in poverty. Clement of Alexandria, as we have
seen, even addressed the more pointed question of how a rich
person can be saved (*Quis Dives Salvetur*). Already in the early
years of Christianity the social and demographic character
of the church was in flux, requiring theologians and leaders
to formulate new ways of articulating what the Christian life
demanded. Likewise, as each of us moves through the life
cycle, we need to stay current with the church's developing
teachings and their meaning for our lives. That must include
the moral teachings on possessions and wealth in a world
increasingly marked by scarcity.

### Practice Generosity

Financial stewardship must become for each of us a virtue—that is, a good habit of generously sharing the resources
at our disposal. It does require effort, practice, and commitment if we are to give for the right reason. That proper motivation is not public recognition, not our name on a building,
but thanksgiving for what we already have received.

In practicing financial stewardship in relation to our faith
community we need to remember that our parish may not
always be what we would like it to be. Every congregation
is made up of people with many different expectations, and
sometimes with pastoral leaders who don't measure up to our

particular expectations. No parish is perfect and every one of them makes mistakes as do families, workplaces, and the other communities to which we belong.

Our parish reflects the human sinfulness, brokenness, and shortcomings of its members. We are not always what God expects us to be, yet he continues to love us in spite of our failures. And so must we imitate this loving, forgiving, and supportive attitude in our response to our own parish. We practice this virtue, this good habit, of financial stewardship not because the parish is doing everything right, but because it is seeking to carry out the mission of Jesus Christ by proclaiming the good news, by celebrating God's presence, by forming us into a community that reflects God's love and compassion to a hurting world. Could there be a better cause or program for us to support? We practice financial stewardship also because sharing our resources opens the door to our deeper engagement in the life of the church, and to our conversion.

## Note

1. Gregory of Nyssa, *On the Love of the Poor,* in Peter C. Phan, *Social Thought,* Message of the Fathers of the Church 20 (Wilmington, DE: Michael Glazier, 1984), 132.